Asphalt Warrior

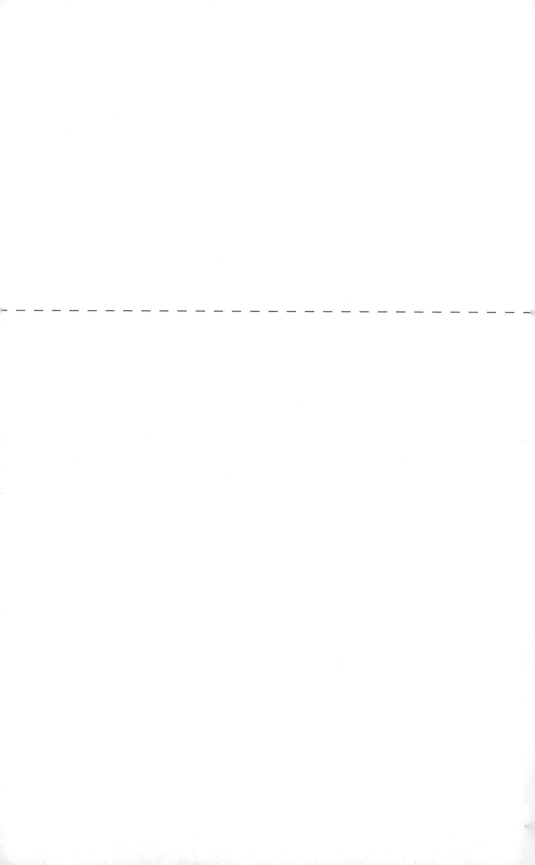

OTHER BOOKS BY KURT BOONE

Looking for Myself

POEMS

Introduction by Noreen Mallory

Inside Grand Central Terminal

A PHOTO ESSAY

Photography by John Sarsgard

New York Alleycats: Photography by Amy Bolger

Co-authored with Kevin Bolger

Illustrations by Greg Ugalde

On the Subway

POEMS

Illustrations by Greg Ugalde and Jeff Hill

Urban Theory: Critical Thoughts in America (ebook)

Co-authored with Noreen Mallory

Perspective by Stephanie Wilson, PhD

Messenger Poet

Illustrations by Greg Ugalde

Asphalt Warrior

THE STORY OF NEW YORK CITY'S FASTEST MESSENGER

KURT BOONE

TASORA BOOKS

First published in the United States of America by Kurt Boone Books, 2011

ISBN 978-1-934690-29-1

Printed in the United States of America

Set in Paperback / Designed by Mark Melnick

Photo credits: Amy Bolger (p. 4, 63, 64); John Sarsgard (p. 98, 122); Jason Felker (pp. 48–49); Wilis K. Johnson (p. 71); Ron Herard (p. 74);

TASORA BOOKS
5120 Cedar Lake Road, Minneapolis, MN 55416
Distributed by Itasca Books

Contents

Introduction   11

Rapid Messenger Service   21
Excel Messenger Service   27
Kangaroo Couriers   31
Rapid Courier 225 Bicycle Company   37
Bicycle Messengers, Foot Messengers, Dispatchers,
    Owners and Wannabees   41
Mobile Parcel Carriers   47
    "The Rush for Dr. Konaldi"   65
    "Mary Howard Studio"   66
    "City Tidbits"   68
    "Subway Stories"   70
Skyscrapers, Doormen and 9/11   75
Entrepreneurial Spirit   83

Messenger Poet   99

ATTORNEY GENERAL
VISITOR PASS
09/17/10

Kurt Boone
Host Information:
24FL M' CLERKS
mail

Time In: | Valid Thru
4:02:09 | 14:30:00

HBO

Delivery

KURT BOONE

6/24/2008 **C Level**

Kurt
Boone

9/23/2009

Host | 5t
Escort Pa

SLG

2 Wall Street

VISITOR

boone kurt

Visiting:
Receptionist Default
Ceccarelli Weprin PLLC

4/2010 **7TH FLOOR**

79 Madison Ave

GVA Williams

02/25/10
05:46 pm
Meeting
6fl CHN

Kurt Boone
Mobile Mess

Lobby Station

1114 Avenue of the Americas

VISITOR
kurt boone

Visiting:
NHCLC

5/2/2008 - Concourse

2/5/2010

G
/10

BOONE
late General of Brazil

1065 Ave

9/22/201

COURIER

BOONE KURT
INDIMESS

Van Eck

ANTHIS T
REALTY CORP.

Kurt Boone
2009.9.28 at 13:39:00 PM
16th Flr - NYCC
Company:

250 BROADWAY

04

et
KURT E

MOBI

Visitor

Park Avenue
GUEST
Kurt Boone
Mobile Messenger

8/4/2009   **3RD FLOOR**

---

295 Madison Avenue

KURT BOONE

04/29/09   11:20 am

120953

---

the Americas
03/17/10

urt boone
enger Center
n Area: /Cellar

750
d Ave.
EST
t Boone
N/A
FLOOR

New York City Transit   ***VISITOR'S PASS***
130 Livingston Plaza

Guest : KURT BOONE

Floor : 10 FLOOR

Host : D WALLEN 37095 VIDE

Ext. :3418

Expires : 10/2/2008
Please return this pass to the Security Desk in the 1st floor lobby

---

100 Church Street
VISITOR

K BOONE
N/A

Visiting:
Niche Media
Jason Binn

2/8/2010   **7th Floor**

---

99 Park Ave.
VISITOR
07/13/10   17:18:15

Kurt Boone

Destination

Main Lobby

KURT
BOONE
05/21/10
15:21:23

Americas
ITOR
Boone
IA

Radio Networks, Inc.

FLOOR

1155 Avenue of the Americas

VISITOR

Kurt Boone, Mobile Messenger
Visiting: White & Case
Cellar (C-1)

August 14, 2009

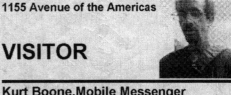

5/10

7

URIER

750
Third Ave.
GUEST

DAILY MANIFEST

1E _____ DATE_____ DAY _____ PAGE

DELIVERY LOCATION	REMARKS	RECEIVED IN GOOD CONDITION
PANY:_____ R:_____ FL:	N.P.U._____RUSH_____ WAIT TIME_____ #PIECES_____O/S_____ WEIGHT_____ C.O.D. AMT:_____	SIGNATURE PRINT NAME
PANY:_____ R:_____ FL:	N.P.U._____RUSH_____ WAIT TIME_____ #PIECES_____O/S_____ WEIGHT_____ C.O.D. AMT:_____	SIGNATURE PRINT NAME
PANY:_____ _____ FL:	N.P.U._____RUSH_____ WAIT TIME_____ #PIECES_____O/S_____ WEIGHT_____ C.O.D. AMT:_____	SIGNATURE PRINT NAME
PANY:_____ R:_____ FL:	N.P.U._____RUSH_____ WAIT TIME_____ #PIECES_____O/S_____ WEIGHT_____ C.O.D. AMT:_____	SIGNATURE PRINT NAME
PANY:_____ R:_____ FL:	N.P.U._____RUSH_____ WAIT TIME_____ #PIECES_____O/S_____ WEIGHT_____ C.O.D. AMT:_____	SIGNATURE PRINT NAME
PANY:_____ R:_____ FL:	N.P.U._____RUSH_____ WAIT TIME_____ #PIECES_____O/S_____ WEIGHT_____ C.O.D. AMT:_____	SIGNATURE PRINT NAME
PANY:_____ R:_____ FL:	N.P.U._____RUSH_____ WAIT TIME_____ #PIECES_____O/S_____ WEIGHT_____ C.O.D. AMT:_____	SIGNATURE PRINT NAME
PANY:_____ R:_____ FL:	N.P.U._____RUSH_____ WAIT TIME_____ #PIECES_____O/S_____ WEIGHT_____ C.O.D. AMT:_____	SIGNATURE PRINT NAME
PANY:_____ R:_____ FL:	N.P.U._____RUSH_____ WAIT TIME_____ #PIECES_____O/S_____ WEIGHT_____ C.O.D. AMT:_____	SIGNATURE PRINT NAME
PANY:_____ R:_____	N.P.U._____RUSH_____	

Introduction

LIFE AS A NEW YORK CITY MESSENGER ALWAYS SEEMS
to be on the edge. Young people running and cycling in and around
New York City traffic during business hours is a feat unto itself. But
make no mistake about it the messenger business is serious, if not
dead serious. New York City is often called the business capital of
the world. As a foot messenger I live and breathe this energy every
minute and second of the business day in Manhattan, and throughout
the city on occasion.

As a former track star in the city, I was hired as a messenger because
I could move very fast. In my 14 years as a messenger I have been hit
by a car only once: I was hit by a cab door swinging open in front of
Trump Towers, but I wasn't hurt—in fact, the person who opened the
door didn't even know he hit me. People walk on the sidewalks very
quickly in New York City. In my case, I walked three times or four
times as fast as most people on the sidewalk. Many people say they
don't see the foot messengers, they only see bicycle messengers, but
that is because the foot messengers are that fast. Our symbol could
be the fleet-footed messenger god Mercury of the Romans (known
as Hermes in Ancient Greece), flying along with wings on our heels.

By the time I finished high school, I had garnered considerable
attention and accolades for my skills as a runner. In 1976, I won the

Police Athletic League 115-pound New York City Long Jump Championship. I trained with the Police Athletic League Elite girls' track team summer practice squad, coached by Norman Tate, a member of the USA Triple Jump Team in the 1968 Mexico City Olympics, where I believe Coach Tate took fourth place in the Triple Jump.

It was also in high school that I and my brother Bruce picked up a very useful skill from my father: knowing how to read maps and learning the city streets. Often times after a track meet somewhere in the city, far from where we lived in Jamaica, Queens, or after track practice with the PAL elite girls team in the Washington Heights section of Manhattan, Bruce and I would explore the streets of Manhattan. We would travel to downtown Manhattan, Greenwich Village, Soho, Harlem and even explore the South Bronx.

In addition to track meets and practices, we were doing vendor jobs at Shea Stadium and Yankee Stadium. Figuring out which buses and trains to take from Jamaica, Queens to Shea Stadium and Yankee Stadium would give me and Bruce even more streetwise skills. At Yankee Stadium and Shea Stadium, we would join our other brothers Elliott and Frederick Boone. Vending work was great money in high school, allowing me and my brothers to buy and wear the latest fashions.

My father, Elliott Boone, Sr., worked the graveyard shift at the General Post Office on 34th Street in Manhattan. He told me stories about his co-workers who did messenger work to make extra money. The messenger work my father was talking about was mainly foot messenger work. To my father, the bicycle messenger business was dangerous. The early streetwise lessons and stories about messenger work from my father, coupled with advertisements in the local newspapers for track stars to become messengers on commission, attracted me to the messenger business.

My first mail room experience came from a LaGuardia Community College internship at United Artists/MGM my freshman year. The job was for an indoor messenger. I wore a blue MGM blazer and was responsible for delivering and picking up the mail on all 17 floors of the MGM Building. The MGM headquarters where I worked was located at 729 7th Avenue in Manhattan. I was only in that mailroom job for 3 months, basically completing my internship and then dropping out of college to work in a juvenile crime prevention organization.

So, in September of 1978, a year after graduating from High School in 1977, I was involved with trying to stop the spread of youth violence in my neighborhood. For all intents and purposes Jamaica, Queens where I lived wasn't a ghetto. It was a middle- and upper-middle-class African-American community. Sadly, however, gang culture, drug dealing and youth violence was increasing in the neighborhood. This was a time before the black-on-black crime wave and the crack cocaine epidemic.

I partnered with Charles Fisher, the president of Counselors of Positive Progress (now called Youth Enterprises). I was the vice-president of COPP and I spoke out where I could about preventing youth violence and juvenile delinquency. Charles and I were also members of the Five Percent Nation of Islam, but that's another story. Like everyone else at that time, while working with COPP, I was smoking marijuana, so in a way what I was doing was a contradiction. But to many people, smoking marijuana was no more harmful than drinking beer or vodka, except that smoking and selling marijuana was illegal.

Having second thoughts about whether I had made the right decision to quit college and work in my community, I resigned from COPP. In any event, I wanted to move on with my young life. But truth be told, it was later on in my adult life that black-on-black crime and drug addition would become epidemic in the black community nationwide, with crime and punishment touching my family and millions of other black families.

In 2010 as I write this introduction, I am fifty years old, having completed 14 years working as a messenger, and still single. I have relatives who have been murdered, put in jail for crimes they have committed, and one who died from AIDS. With that said, I also have many other relatives who went on to become extremely successful. Just as we have experienced the first Black President in Barack Obama, my generation is continuing the legacy our ancestors left us. However, I always wanted to be married and have kids. If you want to know my biggest tragedy, it is that I still do not have my own family.

After resigning from COPP I drifted into a few different jobs and eventually decided to join the Navy. My last job in the city was as a messenger for Walter Kaye, after which I went into the Navy the winter of 1982. Basic training was at the US Naval Training Center in Great Lakes, Illinois. I didn't stay that long in the Navy and was discharged honorably in four months. I served as my company athletic petty officer, because I was basically the best all-around athlete in my company. I was discharged for lying on my application that I never used drugs before.

After my discharge from the Navy, I came back to New York City for a few months, then decided to go to Los Angeles, CA. I lived in Los Angeles for 6 years, obtained an Associate Degree in Business Administration and 100 credits towards my bachelor degree. By the time I got back to New York City in 1988. I was 28, had an A.A. degree, had worked as a Radio Shack store manager and a temporary sales associate for AT&T Merlin Telephone Systems. Back in New York City I became an account executive for MetLife and sold over $1 million in life insurance policies my first year. It looked like I was on my way to success.

But something happened at the MetLife office where I worked that caused me to have second thoughts about working in the life insurance industry. I was terminated at MetLife for not making my sales quota. After my termination from MetLife, I was resigned to be an entrepreneur. By age 30 I had worked at two Fortune 500 Companies with no success. I felt that being an entrepreneur was the only way for me to succeed in business and earn enough money to raise a family.

This is when I decided to used my street knowledge in the messenger industry to help me become an entrepreneur. The business I would eventually start, Boone Marketing Company, would specialize in offering marketing and sales consulting services to minority-owned businesses, primarily African-American-owned businesses.

So I answered an ad in the *New York Post* from Rapid Messenger Service looking for foot messengers. I was hired for part-time work on commission by manager Ed Harrington. In high school I could run the 100 yard dash in 10 seconds. Ten seconds was a very competitive track time in New York City and nationally. My high school track success was hampered by not being truly healthy, because of the circumstances in my middle-class neighborhood with gangs, drug culture and youth confusion. But this running speed would serve me well as a messenger for Rapid Messenger Service.

At Rapid Messenger Service I began to learn many parts of the city. Dispatchers at Rapid Messenger Service sent me everywhere, from downtown Manhattan to uptown Manhattan, to Brooklyn, The Bronx, Queens and Staten Island. I got to see parts of the city firsthand, and it was an amazing and exciting experience. Though the pay wasn't that much, the experience was beyond belief. It was as if I were the mayor of New York City, visiting countless neighborhoods on the campaign trail.

In early 1990s, entering and leaving the hundreds of skyscrapers around the city was security-free. As a messenger, you could enter some of the city biggest and most famous skyscrapers without a security team checking you out. I would go into the Chrysler Building, Empire State Building, Woolworth Building and up to the 109th floor, one of the highest floors in the World Trade Center Twin Towers, without security checking my bag or seeing if I had a messenger ID card. In fact, Rapid Messenger Service never gave me or other messengers working there ID cards. The only proof we were messengers were the messenger pickup and delivery tickets we carried for our jobs.

As a foot messenger in the early 1990s, I would see the very fast bicycle messengers pass me by all the time on the city streets. I didn't know any of them until later in my messenger life, because Rapid Messenger Service did not use bicycle messengers. At Rapid Messenger Service I also learned how to work with van driver messengers as a helper. There were thousands of van driver messengers throughout the city. Getting a helper job with a driver was weird. One minute you were rushing a package to somewhere in the city and the next minute dispatch would tell you to help a driver lift heavy boxes or move furniture. You would have to adjust from agile speed to physical strength at a moment's notice . . . though I must say the van driver messenger helper jobs paid extremely well.

The period when I worked at Rapid Messenger Service was also the time I began to see many communities, people and cultures that called New York City home. Though I did not realize it at the time, because I took the American Dream for granted, people from every corner on earth come to New York City seeking freedom and economic empowerment. As an African American and a descendant of American slavery, I took freedom somewhat lightly. I think because my parents experienced Jim Crow laws in the south and racism in the north, I was apprehensive about fully embracing the American Dream. But these other folks from different countries where freedom was limited or non-existent viewed New York City and America as the greatest opportunity to mankind in 20th Century.

From 1990-1994, and then again becoming a messenger in 2000 to the present, I had deliveries to some of the most well-known places in the city, like Lincoln Center, The Metropolitan Museum of Art, Park Avenue apartment buildings. Doormen would open the gilded doors so I could enter some the spectacular foyers of some of the richest residential buildings in the world. Rush packages had to be carried through Chinatown, Little Italy, Harlem, Soho, Greenwich Village, the South Bronx, Long Island City, Jersey City and as far away as

Brighton Beach, Coney Island and Staten Island. I rode the trains a lot and walked 8 to 12 miles a day all year long. On many train rides, I would write poetry to pass the time. My poetry was about articles I read in the newspapers, television news, city living, black love, hip hop culture, messenger worked or whatever I had on my mind. I went on to have several books of poetry published, including "Looking for Myself," "On the Subway" and "Messenger Poet".

Using messenger work to support my goal of becoming an entrepreneur, I found myself in the film business. While at Rapid Messenger Service, I worked with Spike Lee, Denzel Washington and Angela Bassett as an extra in the film "Malcolm X". I was paid $50.00 a day for three days, and my face as an extra in the movie was seen worldwide.

After four years at Rapid Messenger Service, I got a job as an Avon Independent Sales Representative. I went on to sell Avon for six years, selling over $200,000 worth of Avon Products. Towards the end of my fifth year selling Avon Products, my sales began to decline for some reason, and eventually I had to close my Avon business and go back to messenger work full time.

Before I left Rapid Messenger Service in 1994, I was considered the fastest foot messenger in the company. As before, I went to the classified section in a local newspaper to find work as a messenger. I answered an ad from Excel Messenger Service to be a part-time foot messenger in 2000. At Excel Messenger Service I got hired by Ovidio Sanabria, office manager and dispatcher. At Excel Messenger Service it would be the first time I worked with bicycle messengers. This led to some important collaborations, both in business and in my book publishing, when I wrote the introduction to "New York Alleycats", photography by Amy Bolger, Epilogue by Kevin Bolger, and illustrations by Greg Ugalde, who also provided illustrations for my "Messenger Poet".

While working the streets of New York City as a courier for Excel Messenger Service, I saw quite a few people, children included, carrying messenger bags. In the case of high school and college kids, I saw them wearing a messenger-looking street wardrobe. This was my first inkling about a growing trend called "Messenger Style". The messenger look consisted of denim pants that have a worn or torn look. For us real messengers, our jeans are really worn because they get damaged from the elements of the street and all kinds of weather conditions. Real messengers wore hoodies, baseball caps, beanies and sneakers to work, not for fashion. In the case of bicycle messengers, many have the foot messenger look which I just described but a lot of bicycle messengers also wear bicycle gear with tailored cycling pants, helmets, jackets, jerseys and bicycle cleats. But what I think made the messenger look so trendy is that most messengers have their own unique look. This inspired fashion designers because there is no limit to what you can create.

As an entrepreneur, I thought this was a gold mine for my business career. So while I was still working at Excel Messenger Service, I started a company called the Messenger 841 Project. The *Messenger 841 Project* was to be a streetwear design firm inspired by the foot and bicycle messengers of New York City.

After September 11, I moved on from Excel Messenger Service to another messenger company called Kangaroo Couriers. But before leaving Excel Messenger Service I was again considered the fastest foot messenger in the company.

At Kangaroo Couriers nothing much changed except I made a little more money. I was also into my second year of the *Messenger 841 Project*. As the messenger bag craze exploded, it seemed that everyone was carrying a messenger bag from Wall Street executives to millionaire internet entrepreneurs to school kids going to school. As a foot messenger who traveled all over the city, I had first-hand experience witnessing the trend. The messenger style grew and continues up to today, and inspired some of the streetwear for skateboarders and other trendsetters. Even Jack Bauer of "24" uses a messenger bag!

But for *Messenger 841 Project*, the road would be difficult, with no capital or outside investors. It was hard to cash in on the trend despite my deep personal knowledge and experience of messenger culture. At Kangaroo Courier I would again become one of their favorite messengers because of my speed and knowledge of the city. Eventually, however, I would need to move on again to another messenger company for higher pay.

This time I went to a company called Mobile Parcel Carriers, located in the Hell Kitchen section of Manhattan. Mobile Parcel Carriers offer their foot messengers $300.00 to $700.00 a week on a commission basis. In addition, Mobile Parcel Carriers had a reputation for having some of the fastest and best bicycle messengers in New York City. So around April of 2003, I began working at Mobile Parcel Carriers. At Mobile Parcel Carriers my messenger world would be turned upside down. I would experience New York City in the most unique way imaginable.

With my street knowledge and Mobile dispatch team. I saw almost every aspect of city living in New York City. From the bums and subway musicians on the trains, to super rich apartment buildings on the upper east side and west side of Manhattan, to movie studios in the city, hundreds of different neighborhoods, fancy department stores and corner bodegas, riding 22 subway lines a week, working with legendary bicycle messengers, hanging out at bicycle messenger Alleycats parties, writing books about the messenger life, having a documentary film made about my life as a messenger, expanding the *Messenger 841 Project* with licenses from manufacturers, having my own t-shirt souvenir company and eventually having a signature messenger bag in my name made by Seagull Bags.

At Mobile Parcel Carrier I would also maintain a scrapbook of famous people I delivered packages and documents to, like former U.S. President Bill Clinton, Yoko Ono, Judith Jamison, Rachel Ray, Wyclef Jean, television and movie production offices for the "Sopranos", "Fringe" and "The Taking of Pelham 1,2,3." Also the backstage of Lincoln Center, my biggest messenger client over the years; I must have done over 500 deliveries just for the Lincoln Center Complex. On Broadway I delivered to just about all of the backstages from August Wilson Theatre to all the theatres run by the Shubert Organization. At Mobile Parcel Carriers I also did many runs for Alvin Ailey, high fashion companies like Fendi, Ralph Lauren, Gucci and Manolo Blahnik, to deliveries for upscale guests at the Plaza Hotel, Waldorf Astoria, Mandarin Oriental, to residents of the super rich apartment buildings located at 740 Park Avenue, The Dakota, 10 Gracie Square and River House.

All in all, I have become legendary as one of the fastest foot messengers in New York City history, and in that role I have seen some of the highest and lowest aspects of life in New York City. Beyond my messenger work, I have strived to achieve greatness in business, with my *Messenger 841 Project*, and as a writer, with several books of poetry and books about the messenger life, including this one. With that said, in addition to the many stories about city life that I have experienced as a messenger, I have include some tidbits about New York that city dwellers and even visitors might find useful, like little-known public spaces, unique city parks and scenic Manhattan walkways. I may be going too fast to enjoy them most of the time when I'm delivering packages, but you can slow down and appreciate the scenery!

Rapid Messenger Service

AFTER LEAVING JOHN HANCOCK FINANCIAL SERVICES as an independent insurance broker, I knew I had to become an entrepreneur. I wasn't being successful in corporate America. With an Associates Degree in business administration from Los Angeles City College, I had worked as manager of a Radio Shack Store, a temp for AT&T sales executives, an account executive with MetLife and finally as a sales rep with John Hancock Financial Services—all before 32 years of age. After working for John Hancock Financial Services, I became a safe driver for Domino Pizza. While working at Domino Pizza part-time, I decided to look for another job during the day.

Since I had been a former track and field star at Andrew Jackson High School located in Cambria Heights, Queens, I was really fast. I also knew the New York City streets and subway system fairly well. As I mentioned before, New York City Messenger companies were always advertising in the daily newspapers looking for fast runners to be messengers who would work on commission. In 1990, I responded to an ad in the *New York Post* looking to hire experienced messengers, and met with Ed Harrington, the manager and one of dispatchers for Rapid Messenger Service on West 27th Street between 6th and 7th Avenues. Ed hired me that same day. I thought that my time at Rapid Messenger Service would be short. Little did I know I would be working at Rapid Messenger Service for 4 years and most of that work would eventually be full time.

At the same time I started with Rapid Messenger Service, I continued to work evenings for Domino Pizza at the Hollis Avenue and St. Francis Blvd. location in Queens. It was clear to me that I needed to develop a business of my own.

In the early 1990s, African-American filmmakers were becoming successful with independent movies, so I decided to look into opportunities in the movie industry. I had some headshots made and attached my athletic resume to the picture. Damon Smith, an acting friend of mine, told me that Spike Lee was casting for "Malcolm X" through Robi Reed & Associates. I sent my headshot to Robi Reed and was called to be cast as a paid extra in Spike Lee's "Malcolm X". The extra acting job was to sit next to Angela Bassett for 3 days in the assassination scene on the stage set of Audubon Ballroom, when Malcolm X, played by Denzel Washington, was assassinated.

I was working three jobs at this time, and I needed all three jobs, because altogether they still didn't pay enough money to live on, even though I was staying at home, paying my mother and father a weekly rent.

On Christmas Day I got into an accident with my car, a Nissan Sentra, which was totally destroyed. I survived unharmed, because the car was hit on the empty passenger side of the vehicle. That accident ended my worked for Domino Pizza, and I became a full-time foot messenger for Rapid Messenger Service.

As a full-time messenger for Rapid Messenger Service I had to work very hard to pay my bills. Rapid Messenger Service only paid a piecework commission per delivery, no base salary. Rapid Messenger Service had been in business since 1929. It was started by Peter Matthew's father, who left the business to him to manage and own. Peter Matthew was a young white boy who graduated from the University of Miami, if my memory serves me right.

In any case, Peter blended in with the messengers, even doing messenger runs himself if a messenger wasn't available. Rapid Messenger Service (like most other messenger services) employed a mixed group of people as messengers: There were college graduates like me, college students, ex-convicts, misfits who needed a job and individuals who owned vans for truck runs. Our address was 149 West 27th Street in Manhattan.

A typical day would be from 8:00am to 6:00pm. My dispatchers at Rapid Messenger Service were Ed Harrington, senior dispatcher and manager, Purcell and Maria who wrote up the messenger jobs and then would give them to either Ed, Purcell and sometimes Peter who would also dispatch on occasion.

At Rapid Messenger Service we had three rate cards, billed under the names Rapid Messenger Service, Rush Couriers and Insured Messenger. Each rate sheet had a different color ticket. My courier code was the number 225. Dispatchers would rarely call us by name for work, just using our messenger number. The messenger rate charge was determined by what service a client was billed for.

At Rapid Messenger Service, messengers were paid a commission of 50% per job ticket completed. We were told how much each job run was worth and thus new how much commission we earned each day and week. We were paid every week by check from all of the jobs we did that week. Since there were rarely any tips paid for being a messenger, extra money for me would come from tokens we would receive to ride the train to a delivery or pickup. Since it was sometimes faster to walk than wait for the train, in a good week I could collect over 20 subway tokens, then cash them in at a MTA token booth for cash.

One of our biggest accounts at Rapid Messenger Service was Essence Magazine. We also did work for BET's New York Office. At that time Rapid Messenger Service had no radios or beepers, and no one had cell phones yet. Either we would get 4 or 5 jobs at once from dispatch when we came into the office, or we would use a pay telephone to call dispatch for more work or to report any problems. These phone calls were expenses for messengers, and we were not reimbursed for these pay phone calls. If not managed properly, these calls could make your commissions earned drop below minimum wage. At Rapid Messenger Service, after expenses, I was averaging about $6.00/hr.

During downtime in the office, we messengers talked about everything from gang life, newspaper headlines, sports and just plain everyday life in New York City. Some of the most popular discussions were about Rap Music and Urban Street Fashion, two youth movements growing in popularity. The successes and tragedies from Hip Hop culture were all around us, from the Bronx, where dispatcher Ed Harrington grew up, to Hollis, Queens where I live.

When making pickups or deliveries for Jive Records, Atlantic Records and Universal Records, we all personally experienced the growth of Hip Hop Culture. We had D-Jays, break dancers, poets and graffiti artists among the messengers at Rapid Messenger Service and throughout the New York City Messenger industry. Urban fashion was also a big topic at Rapid Messenger Service, because messengers were fashion heads, too. Whether it was rocking the latest Nike, Puma or Adidas sneakers or wearing the hottest Hip Hop fashion, New York City messengers were doing it big time.

Some of the new Urban fashion lines that messengers were wearing and discussing all time on the job were Phat Farm, FUBU, Cross-Colors and Mecca. These urban fashion lines were just starting out; urban fashion wasn't the billion-dollar industry it is today. At Rapid Messenger Service and other messenger service companies, the way you looked, dressed and speed of your pickup and deliveries could determine your respect as a New York City messenger.

Rapid Messenger Service did not use bicycle messengers because the owner didn't want to pay the city fees for having bicycle messengers, or deal with the other issues with bicycle messengers. This policy dated back to the beginning of the company.

Also while at Rapid Messenger Service I continue my pursuit of being a freelance writer. I finished one of my poetry book project and got it published with Dorrance Publishing Company in 1994 with financial backing from Mike Rayals, a friend of my brother's, who was a correction officer. My brother and Mike worked at Fishkill State Prison. The book was entitled "Looking For Myself," poetry by Kurt Boone and Introduction by Noreen Mallory. "Looking For Myself" was poetry about growing up in New York City. Noreen Mallory was a freelance writer from Philadelphia that I met at a Black Filmmaker Foundation Writers Workshop held at New York University. Some of the poems in the book I wrote about messenger life, but most of them I wrote in college.

At Rapid Messenger Service I continue seeking new career opportunities. In my third year working for Rapid Messenger Service I came across advertisement in the newspaper to become independent Sales Representative for Avon Products. My next door neighbor and my mother's friend, Ms. Torrance, had sold Avon Products for years, so I was curious to learn what Avon Products was all about. My interview was in the Jamaica Avon office with Mary Poinson, who was a district manager. Ms. Poinson explained what an Avon sales position was and how the commission structure worked. She had also worked with Ms. Torrance, my mother's friend. I then paid $20.00 to open an Avon Products Sales Representative account, and I began working for Avon Products in 1994.

In this Avon Products opportunity I was lucky in the sense that Peter and Ed at Rapid Messenger Service let me sell Avon Products to receptionists on my messenger pickups and deliveries. In my last few months with Rapid Messenger Service, my Avon Products sales were matching or exceeding my messenger commissions, and thus I slowly got tired of messenger work—to the point where I left a package at the Atlantic Record office without obtaining a signature, and went home without telling dispatch what I had done. Peter Matthew got mad at that decision and fired me the next day. Although Ed thought it was okay for me to stay, Pete didn't. So that's how my four years ended at Rapid Messenger Service.

About a year later I learned that Rapid Messenger Service had been sold to another messenger company, and Peter Matthew was no longer in the messenger industry. I became a leading sales representative for Avon Products for 6 years.

Later on, as my Avon Product sales declined, I eventually ended up back in the messenger industry as a foot messenger for Excel Messenger Service.

Excel Messenger Service

AROUND NOVEMBER 2000, MY AVON PRODUCTS SALES were declining. Although I wasn't really interested in doing messenger work again, I was aware that the independence of being a messenger would allow me to continue developing my entrepreneurial projects. By this time I was pursuing my projects under the name Boone Marketing Company. I knew after leaving John Hancock Financial Services as an independent insurance agent in the early 1990's that I would have to employ myself in corporate America.

In any case, I answered an advertisement in a newspaper that said "Messengers Wanted". That advertisement was from Excel Messenger Service, located on the west side of 49th Street in Manhattan's Hell's Kitchen district. Excel Messenger Service was a very small messenger service, owned by a former female messenger, although the actual hiring was done by a manager and dispatcher named Octivia.

I got hired in November 2000 as a part-time foot messenger. Excel Messenger Service paid foot messengers by the hour, bicycle messengers and van drivers by commission. Working at Excel Messenger Service was very tough on the foot messengers. Since foot messengers were paid hourly, there was no incentive or chance to earn a competitive commission wage above the minimum wage that Excel paid. Thus many times my weekly check would fall below minimum wage. This would happen because Excel deducted my taxes and sub-way fare charges from my weekly check. Instead of billing the client for subway charges, Excel billed the messenger.

At that time, the minimum wage was $5.15/hour. As an example, let's say I worked 20 hours a week, earning $103.00. With state and federal taxes deducted, and then a weekly subway metro card of $20.00 deducted, my weekly check could drop down to $70.00 for 20 hours of work—meaning I earned $3.50/hour as a part-time mes-senger.

While at Excel Messenger Service, I started questioning myself about the reasons I was still working as a messenger. I had a college degree with significant corporate work experience, and yet I wasn't pulling down job offers or assignments. My focus was on marketing and sales, with a special interest in developing African-American minority owned businesses. I wanted to use my Fortune 500 experi-ence and help African-American businesses with their marketing and sales efforts, but these opportunities to work with African-American entrepreneurs in publishing, film and fashion were limited, and it was hard to get started with them for a number of reasons. Therefore, continuing to work as a messenger, since it offered steady income (no matter how small) seemed to be a reasonable decision.

At times I would think the difficulties of being an African-American entrepreneur were due to racism, because many African-American entrepreneurs were being denied contracts, financing and other business resources to be successful in corporate America. That said, I asked GOD for help, as well as thinking hard about my situation. And I said to myself, "GOD made me a messenger for some reason. I have to figure out what it is."

Then one day on my way to work at Excel Messenger Service, walk-ing up 49th Street between 8th and 9th Avenue, it hit me: young people and students were emulating the authentic street chic of a New York City Messenger by carrying messenger bags to work and school as a fashion statement. They were carrying messenger bags to say, "I'm streetwise."

Urban street fashion was exploding in the apparel marketplace in 2000, with urban clothing companies earning billion of dollars. Street wear brands like Karl Kani, FUBU, Mecca USA, Cross Colours, Phat Farm and designer labels like Tommy Hilfiger, Polo Jean Co., Calvin Klein Jeans and DKNY were being worn by street kids, copying their favorite Hip Hop stars and Rock n Roll stars who were wearing the hottest street fashions on MTV and BET Videos. Street culture fashion was expanding away from traditional skate and surf wear street culture to a new fashion style, driven from urban neighborhoods across the country, with none greater than New York City.

With this new urban streetwear trend in my mind, I said maybe this is my calling, to design an authentic messenger-style brand of clothing. So I took my messenger number 841 at Excel Messenger Service, and decided to test the fashion world with my clothing design concept called Messenger 841 Project. My family had been in the garment industry already for two generations: my grandmother and my sister's mother-in-law were retirees from International Ladies Garment Worker Union (now called UNITE), and I had been inspired by my years as a messenger for high fashion designers such as Ralph Lauren, Calvin Klein, Donna Karan and others.

I also had many friends from Avon Products who worked on Fashion Avenue, including Sheila Haynes and Linda Logan. Sheila had recently left Calvin Klein and started working for Old Navy, and Linda was a technical designer at Jones Apparel Group. Linda, Sheila and I had networked together in the early days of FUBU, Phat Farm and Cross Colours about developing a fashion brand of our own. But we had no fashion theme to work on, because we weren't involved in Hip-Hop culture and fashion, so our networking never materialized into anything. I reconnected with them and asked them to help me design Apparel for *Messenger 841 Project*. By the summer of 2001, with *Messenger 841 Project* in hand, I was feeling frustrated working for Excel Messenger Service. Not even making the minimum wage was terrible; there just wasn't enough money to live on, much less invest in my own business ideas, and my debts were growing. One of our clients at Excel Messenger Service was Getty Images, the largest photo stock agency in the world. I started making a little extra money by working as night messenger at Getty Images for 1 hour a day, from 6:00pm to 7:00pm at 75 Varick Street or 200 Hudson Street.

Then, on the morning of September 11, I was at home watching Squawk Box on CNBC when a plane hit one of the towers at World Trade Center, just block away from Getty Images office at 200 Hudson Street. Then a few minutes later another plane hit the second tower at World Trade Center. It was all surreal.

If the planes had come around 1:00pm that afternoon, I would possibly have been working at the place they now call Ground Zero. At 1:00pm I was usually stationed outside at 75 Varick to wait for messenger jobs coming from Getty Images, oftentimes waiting for hours even though there was no work. But for sure as a night messenger at Getty Images by 6:00pm, I would have been at Ground Zero, the site of the World Trade Center bombing: 75 Varick Street and 200 Hudson Street is less than a quarter of a mile from where the World Trade Center used to stand.

From that day on, my days at Excel Messenger Service were numbered; I just couldn't get by earning below minimum wage pay anymore.

Kangaroo Couriers

AFTER SEPTEMBER 11, 2001, I LEFT EXCEL MESSENGER
Service and did a short temporary job at Macy's Herald Square as a
stock clerk during the Christmas season. I would begin the New Year
at Kangaroo Couriers.

Kangaroo Couriers was not very different from Excel Messenger Service, except that it offered a minimum wage guarantee plus
commission. This meant that if your commission for the week was
less than minimum wage, Kangaroo Courier would pay you minimum
wage for the week and split your Metrocard fee 50/50 (that is, Kangaroo Courier paid $10.00 and I paid $10.00 to purchase a $20.00
Metrocard). Kangaroo Couriers also didn't use bicycle messengers
while I was there, but did have van drivers as well as foot messengers.

The average commission job at Kangaroo Couriers was $6.00 a run,
and they paid 50% commission, so each job paid around $3.00 a run.
Most days, I would do 12 to 18 runs for Kangaroo Couriers, completing
80-100 jobs per week. While some runs were more or less than $6.00,
my weekly check at Kangaroo averaged $240.00 a week, minus taxes
and subway fee. Most commission-paying messenger companies tell
you what each job cost, so that the messenger and the owner would
know how much commission you earned each week. At Kangaroo
Couriers the option to know what each job cost had been waived by

messengers before I was hired. This was explained to us by the two owners of Kangaroo Couriers during orientation. Therefore, at the end of the week you would know how many runs you made, but not how much commission you had earned. Before you began to work at Kangaroo Couriers, you had to agree to this method of commission earnings. So the only way to guess what your commission for the week might be was to use the average job price of $6.00, as the owners also explained in their orientation.

At Kangaroo Couriers, messengers also had to pay for their own telephone expense to call dispatch to check in and find out the next job pickup instructions. At Excel Messenger Service they gave you a free radio. New York City business districts have thousands of pay telephones, and messenger company owners made full use of that to their advantage. Making messengers pay their own telephone expense added another deduction from messengers' paychecks. Each messenger company in the city has their own way of charging messengers for telephone services needed to complete messenger jobs, whether using your own quarters for pay telephones, paying for a cell phone or a renting a company radio. Telephone fees were all at the messenger expense.

Kangaroo Couriers was another tough messenger company, demanding that you be fast in picking up and delivering packages within an hour by foot or subway. In this regard, only experienced messengers could survive at Kangaroo Couriers. Rarely did dispatch give me directions from pickup to delivery. Terry, the main Kangaroo Couriers dispatcher as well as Lateef, the other dispatcher, would give you two to three runs on the telephone with no direction, and expect you to run or walk to the pickup point for each job at different addresses and deliver both jobs at different addresses within an hour. And if you began not making your deliveries on time, Terry could tell you to go home for the day. Kangaroo Couriers had a lot of African-American foot messengers who could do the work. No single messenger was that important to the company. At Kangaroo Couriers, Rapid Messenger Service and Excel Messenger Service I had been their fastest foot messenger.

I was continuously looking for ways out of the messenger industry with Boone Marketing Company, but nothing developed. After September 11, 2001, I started falling behind on my personal loans that totaled around $20,000, with the largest credit amount being from Beneficial for $9,000. In the year after September 11, 2001, all my loans would collapse. Since then I have paid off 3 loans and am working on paying off the other four loans. I haven't touched a new credit agreement in 3 years (I'm writing this in 2005).

Kangaroo Couriers had a lot of big clients who took advantage of their flat rate messenger service of $6.00 a run from South Ferry to 125th Street in Harlem. The one client I remember the most is Faith Hope Consolo, a famous New York City real estate broker.

After a year at Kangaroo Couriers, their commission rate was just too small to make enough money a week for me to live on and continue to pay back my outstanding loans of over $17,000, and I still wasn't making any money with Boone Marketing Company in 2002. The few internet deals I had through Boone Marketing Company had also dried up when internet bubble collapsed.

As I mentioned in the previous chapter, back in 2001, while I was working at Excel Messenger Service, I was researching messenger styles as I made pickups and deliveries all over the city. I was curious why messenger bags were so popular. From elementary school children going to school, to fashion forward young people out in the streets, to adults dressed for business and headed to the office, all of them were carrying messenger bags.

Then one day in 2003, while I was working at Kangaroo Couriers, I was browsing through books at Barnes & Noble on 53rd Street and Lexington Avenue, and I came across a book entitled "Messenger Styles", with photographs by Philippe Bialobos, published by Assouline in 2000. The book was photographs of real messengers in their street styles. At that time I didn't know any of the messengers in that book. My only disappointment in the book was that they didn't include any foot messengers in their styles—the idea I had been thinking about doing with the *Messenger 841 Project*.

I began my *Messenger 841 Project* by doing small illustrations for t-shirts in my messenger notebook that I used to keep track of my messenger jobs. I did research on graphic design and t-shirt printers in New York City. I picked Design East, located in Greenwich Village, to help me produce the graphics and printing for my first t-shirts. Jonathan of Design East would take all my illustrations and put them into graphics for t-shirts.

At this point I had been a full time messenger for over 6 years. While I did my messenger work, I also studied New York City tourist t-shirt designs. I always loved the different kinds of t-shirt designs that were available in New York City tourist shops. New York City gets over 20 million visitors a year and does 30 billion dollars in sales from tourism business. So in addition to *Messenger 841 Project* I created a New York City souvenir theme concept and logo called *Kurt Boone Authentic New York* for a collection of t-shirt designs for New York City souvenir stores, and began pitching messenger style ideas at Licensing Shows and the New York International Gift Fair

From research in the licensing industry, I signed a one-year agreement with bCreative for licensing art and concepts from *Messenger 841 Project*, and developed a business relationship with Harris-Sach licensing consultants, also for *Messenger 841 Project*. At the New York International Gift Fair, I met with Sharon Ferguson Hendley of Wildwood Productions, a t-shirt manufacturer, who liked messenger styles. Wildwood Productions licensed two of my zip code designs from the *Kurt Boone Authentic New York* Collection.

While this was going on, I began looking at another messenger service called Mobile Parcel Carriers based in the Hell's Kitchen section

of Manhattan, who offered foot messengers commission opportunities from $300.00 to $700.00 a week. At Mobile, bicycle messenger
were offered $400.00 to $1100.00 a week and van drivers $700.00
to $1400.00 a week. I needed the extra money to help fund some
of my entrepreneurial ventures, and continue to pay off the debts I
had accumulated prior to September 11, 2001. So in early 2003 I left
Kangaroo Couriers and started working for Mobile Parcel Carriers
located on 54th Street between 9th and 10th Avenue in Hell Kitchen
section of Manhattan.

Rapid Courier 225 Bicycle Company

WHILE I WAS STILL WORKING AT KANGAROO COURIERS, I was studying the licensing industry in order to find manufacturers for *Messenger 841* Apparel. In one of my discussions with a licensing agent, the idea of creating a bicycle brand from the Messenger industry came up. I sketched out a logo for Jonathan at Design East called *Rapid Courier 225 Bicycle Company* to address some of themes in bicycle messenger culture. The number 225 had been my courier code at Rapid Messenger Service, which was no longer in business. From that combination of my courier code and Rapid Messenger Service going out of business came the name *Rapid Courier 225 Bicycle Company*.

However, I didn't know too much about building bicycles or bicycle style, so I set out on the weekends to get assistance from bicycle shops to develop an ideal messenger bicycle brand. One bicycle shop I discovered on 9th Avenue and 54th Street was called A New Gen Bicycle Shop, which was a major hangout for some of the top bicycle messengers in New York City, and provided their bicycle supplies. They also promoted bike messenger fashion and style. I talked with Angelo Betemit, one of the owners of A New Gen, and told him about the idea from a licensing agent of developing a messenger brand bicycle. He like the idea and agreed to work with me on it, and later became an investor in *Messenger 841 Project*.

As I mentioned in the last chapter, I wasn't making enough money at Kangaroo Couriers, so I decided to take a job at Mobile Parcel Carriers (more on that in the next chapter). Mobile Messenger Service had a real big bicycle messenger division that was considered by many other bicycle messengers the fastest and the best, and they offered the highest payable commission rate in the city. At Mobile I started meeting a lot of bicycle messengers.

One of those bicycle messengers was Wil Wiechter. Wil knew a lot about building bicycles, and he also knew a lot of bicycle messengers in the city. I asked Wil to join my team as part owner and founder along with Angelo in development of the *Rapid Courier 225 Bicycle Company* concept. In addition, Wil would also introduce me to the New York Bicycle Messenger Association and the underground world of New York Alleycats. New York Alleycats are bicycle messengers who race each other to see who is the fastest bicycle messenger in the city. It was in this world that I started meeting messengers who were in the "Messenger Styles" book. So Wil, Angelo and I would meet on Saturdays periodically along with Jeff who also worked at A New Gen Bicycle and was a bicycle messenger with over 18 years experience.

In these Saturday meetings we would discuss opportunities that came from my marketing of *Rapid Courier 225 Bicycle Company* concept. The first opportunity was with Cycle Source Group for custom bicycles. I met the Cycle Source Group at the International Toy Fair in New York City. Nyle Nims, the president of Cycle Source Group, liked the concept and was interested in helping us. Through Cycle Source Group we looked at opportunities to manufacture and distribute *Rapid Courier 225 Bicycles* ourselves, paying for production, warehousing and distribution of bicycles on our own. Cycle Source Group manufactured their bicycles' license and custom through a partner in China.

In the second year I was promoting *Rapid Courier 225 Bicycle Company* concept at the International Toy Fair, I asked Wil, Angelo and Kevin "Squid" Bolger (another veteran bicycle messenger and Alleycat racer) to come meet with Nyle Nims of the Cycle Source Group. We met with Nyle Nims but nothing substantial came out of it, and after the meeting, everybody went their own way on show floor.

I continued looking for opportunities from other bicycle manufacturers. While walking the floor I saw Iron Horse Bicycles' exhibit. I immediately got excited because that was one of the popular bicycle brands being sold in A New Gen Bicycle. In the booth was Stewart Barnett, CEO and Sean Gregg, Director of Sales & Marketing for Iron Horse Bicycles.

I mentioned to Stewart Barnett that I was at the show to promote the concept of an authentic bicycle messenger brand through *Rapid Courier 225 Bicycle Company*. I told him one of my partners was Angelo Betemit of A New Gen Bicycle, one of his customers. I said I could bring Angelo and my other partner Wil back to International Toy Fair to discuss the concept with him. Stewart initially like the ideal and agree to meet with me, Angelo and Wil the next day. So I called Angelo and Wil on my cell phone to set up a time. The next day we met with Stewart and he got excited about the project. He next wanted us to meet in his office in Long Island, New York. Angelo couldn't make any meetings and said it would be up to me and Wil to sell the idea. The idea was for me and Wil to convince Iron Horse Bicycles to license our brand and the messenger community of New York City would assist in marketing and sales of the bicycles. The New York Bicycle Messenger Association even allowed us to use their logo in the presentation.

In the first meeting we met with Stewart Barnett, Sean Gregg and their product manager Todd Seplavy. We discussed developing a messenger-style road bike first. Then we thought to set up a second meeting to see if the project was viable. In the end, it turned out that Iron Horse Bicycle decided not to proceed on licensing the concept.

By summer of 2004 I was hanging out with the bicycle messenger community in New York City, where I met messengers from Alleycat scene. I met Tone, Greg Ugalde, Amy Bolger, Jose Morales, Carlos, Victor, Speedy, Hodari, Mike Dee and many others. I started participating in some of their events like Body Glove Messenger Challenge and BMC Software Messenger Race where I sponsored a team for *Rapid Courier 225 Bicycle Company.*

We saw Stewart and Todd of Iron Horse Bicycles at the race, but they had already lost interest in the *Rapid Courier 225 Bicycle Company* concept. A New Gen Bicycle was going to close down and Wil wanted out, too. Angelo invested $500.00 to keep the project going with the bicycle concept as well as the messenger style clothes with Messenger 841. So by the summer of 2006 *Rapid Courier 225 Bicycle Company* was a non-issue and all I had left was my original logo and design from 2003.

In 2007 I produced a book entitled "New York Alleycats" with photography by Amy Bolger, illustrations by Greg Ugalde, and additional text by Kevin Bolger. I still have the rights to *Rapid Courier 225 Bicycle Company* and plan to eventually trademark the logo and continue to market the idea of a bicycle messenger brand owned by the messengers themselves.

Bicycle Messengers, Foot Messengers, Dispatchers, Owners and Wannabees

FIXED-GEAR BICYCLES HAVE BEEN SPREADING AROUND the world like a virus, a craze attributed to bicycle messenger culture. This is a culture developed by working bicycle messengers who have their own fraternity of fun and games. This fraternity of messengers ride bicycles with one speed and no brakes, dubbed "Fixed Gear". Secondly, the fraternity was made of what you wear, that is mainly torn clothes with a distressed look—not because messengers had money to buy high-end street fashion, but because of the brutal beat down clothes can take when you're working as a bicycle messenger in New York City.

Working as a bicycle messenger, you are affected by all the elements of the outdoors, including weather, traffic, and rough streets. You are responsible for the maintenance and upkeep of your bicycle, and carrying your basic equipment which includes a messenger bag, helmet, tool kit, lock and chain. Working as a bicycle messenger is not a casual bike ride through Central Park. If anything, bicycle messenger work is an action sports job with very little pay and many times no health insurance coverage or employment benefits.

When I was in high school, working as a foot messenger was a popular job. It was the equivalent of working at McDonald's or being a file clerk, except you needed to be able to walk really fast, and you had to know the streets of the city. As a foot messenger, dispatchers and messenger company owners send me many places far from the bicycle messenger zones of Manhattan. The bicycle messenger main routes are between Battery Park and 125th Street, about 8 square miles. A foot messenger would be sent to the outer boroughs regularly, often carrying large boxes and bags that a bicycle messenger can't fit into his or her messenger bag. Foot messengers also had their own style. One former foot messenger, Daymond John, started FUBU ("For Us By Us"), one of the first urban street wear brands.

Being a foot messenger requires being streetwise and fast. There are many neighborhoods in the Bronx and Brooklyn that you can get hurt or lost trying to deliver a package. Working as a foot messenger at Mobile, I never know where I was going to be picking up or delivering a package. Just this past week I was in the South Bronx, Flatbush and Brighton Beach. Even though over the years I have not had any problems getting around the city and different neighborhoods doing messenger work, I am acutely aware of what could go wrong. If I got lost or ran into the wrong crowd of people, I know what to do, for I have come across some dangerous looking people in my day and once I even saw a bank robbery in progress. The bank robber ran right by me, which was insane. For my own safety I never act as though I am lost, and always maintain a look of confidence and security.

I only once worked as a bicycle messenger, when dispatch at Mobile Messenger Service asked me to pick up a bicycle and package from a bicycle messenger who had been hit by a car. The bicycle messenger who was hit by the car got into an ambulance and I rode his bicycle to deliver the package and then rode his bicycle to the Mobile Messenger Service dispatch office, where I locked it up and went back to work as a foot messenger.

I didn't meet any bicycle messengers personally when I was working at Rapid Messenger Service from 1990 to 1994, because they didn't have bicycle messengers, just had foot messengers and car/van drivers. I started working with bicycle messengers when I returned to the messenger business in 2000 at Excel Messenger Service . . . and I didn't start hanging out in bicycle messenger culture world until I got to Mobile Messenger Service. By that time I already had 6 years experience as a foot messenger and considered in high regard as one of the fastest in the city. A co-worker, Wil Wiecher, who was a bicycle messenger at Mobile, was well-known in bicycle messenger world. He introduced me to the party scene and bicycle messenger racing called Alleycats.

This scene does not exist in the foot messenger world. This bicycle messenger party scene was intriguing. Upon first entering this world, it seemed that the rest of the messenger industry didn't exist, but the swagger of the messenger did. What I mean by swagger of the messenger is the work decorum. This is when the dispatchers and owners come into play in this thing called the messenger industry. All working messengers in New York City must adhere to tough working orders given out by dispatchers and owners. Owners and dispatchers try (and some do) rule the messenger industry with an iron fist, meaning you follow their orders or quit their particular messenger company. In the bicycle messenger party world I felt a bit odd that your style as a messenger comes from just bicycle messengers only. I have run across bicycle messengers who dislike foot messengers. Many bicycle messengers think foot messengers are lazy, dumb and look stupid. In some cases that may be true, but to dis the whole foot messenger world is crazy.

Don't get this wrong between the world of the foot messenger and bicycle messenger: The bicycle Messenger party scene is about fun and games, and technically, anybody who wants to hang out can, and even non-messengers can race with their bicycles in an Alleycat race. The bicycle messenger party scene is just about open to anyone, except it is not foot messenger or van driving messenger based.

Getting back to the messenger industry and the dispatchers and owners ruling the industry with an iron fist: From my observation (I am not a bicycle messenger), dispatchers and owners do not give preferential treatment to bicycle messengers. Bicycle and Foot messengers are paid at the same rate. The more runs you do, the more you get paid. But because they could cover more ground in the same amount of time, the bicycle and van-driving messengers often earned more overall. For instance the rumor was that foot messengers could make $700.00 a week, bicycle messengers could make $1000.00 a week, drivers could make $1,200.00 a week, dispatchers could make $1,100.00 a week, and owners would gross $200,000 a week in total messenger jobs.

You do the math on who's making the most money here. To me, owners treat bicycle messengers like paper boys. For bicycle messengers there are no bonuses for all the daily dangers they face on the road and in traffic. Many times there is no unemployment or health insurance for bicycle and foot messengers. Many times an owner would fire a bicycle messenger faster than he would a foot messenger. Owners don't care how fast you are on bicycle or if you kill yourself. There is no big death benefit waiting for your family if you get killed as a bicycle messenger. Don't get me wrong, for foot messengers and drivers worked under the same conditions, it's just not quite as dangerous on a day-to-day basis.

Outsiders sometimes come into the messenger world to make movies, design clothes and messenger bags, or hire models. They seem to think that bicycle messengers are the only messengers, but that is a big mistake. The term "wannabees" in the messenger world means bicycle riders wanting to look and possibly act like bicycle messengers. Messenger work in New York City is an edgy job with its own style and swagger. Young people today are attracted to that because messenger work is tough, but it's not the toughness of a criminal or ex-con. To me the so-called wannabees are entrepreneurs that are creating a new culture unto itself, but rooted in messenger culture, from Alleycats racing, to the messenger bag, to the messenger look, to performing tricks on bicycle, or just riding a fixed gear bicycle. I see the wannabees as young entrepreneurs taking advantage of a great opportunity.

In some cases the entrepreneurs who are selling messenger styles are ex-messengers themselves, although from my observation of the people selling messenger styles, 95 percent are people who have never been a messenger. As far as veteran messenger with more than ten years experience, there are none that I have met selling messenger styles—except for a small group of foot and bicycle messengers who I have worked with. I formed the Messenger 841 Project in 2001 to try to bring working veteran messengers into the business of selling messenger styles. Most of the owners and dispatchers don't care about messenger culture. Owners and dispatchers seem to make enough money and see no reason to get into selling messenger styles with their own branded messenger bags and apparel.

The messenger culture business has reached multi-million dollars in sales with brands like Timbuk 2, Manhattan Portage, Bailey Works, Chrome Bags and Crumpler and new brands Reload Bags, Seagull Bags, Freight Baggage, Affinity Cycles and Continuum Cycles. Indirectly there are millions of dollars being made from manufacturing fixed-gear bicycles that is attributed to bicycle messengers culture and style.

Fixed gear bicycle culture could be $100 million dollar business all by itself. The Sony movie "Premium Rush" has a budget of 60 million dollars. Fixed gear bicycle riding has exploded all around the world with blogs, apparel brands, custom frames and fixed gear boutique shops. Most of the entrepreneurs who make money from messenger culture have no idea on the world on which it is based. That is, messenger styles come from a deep, authentic, urban work ethic that is truly found in the messenger dispatch centers of New York City and other cities. The youth, men and women who work in these dispatch offices, consist of bicycle messengers, foot messengers, motorcycle riders, van drivers, dispatchers and owners. Wannabees are nowhere to be found.

All in all, I am excited about the messenger world. There are some great opportunities on the horizon and I believe the messengers themselves will reap the rewards, as we pursue and extend our culture into the world of business, fashion and manufacturing.

Mobile Parcel Carriers

SOMETIMES WHEN I WAS ON A PICKUP OR DELIVERY for Kangaroo Couriers I would pass by a sign on West 54th Street advertising "Messengers Wanted". The sign was placed outside the ground floor office of Mobile Parcel Carriers. Their motto was "We Deliver Anything Anywhere". Mobile Parcel Carriers offered two benefits to messengers like me who wanted freedom and the opportunity to earn high commissions. I was an entrepreneur with many outside interests, so I needed a company that gave me flexible work schedules. At Mobile Parcel Carriers you could work anytime you wanted—and they also paid high commissions for full-time workers.

So I decided to leave Kangaroo Courier and go to worked for Mobile Parcel Carriers. This was around May of 2002. Mobile Parcel Carriers was located on far west side of 54th Street in the Hell's Kitchen neighborhood of Manhattan. The interview process was fast and included watching a video about my responsibilities and commission opportunities as a messenger working for Mobile Parcel Carriers. After I signed the contract as an independent contractor, I started working the same day. Mike, a dispatcher who conducted the orientation, also gave me my courier code. My courier code was 300 Book.

I didn't know much about Mobile Parcel Carriers when I arrived, but I learned quickly that Mobile Parcel Carriers had a history of

HOME OF: "WE DELIV

MOBILE PAR

being one of the fastest messenger services in the city of New York. They have been in the messenger industry since 1971. I heard from other messengers who worked there that the two owners, Dave and Paul, were both former bicycle messengers themselves, along with Forest, Dave's son, who is one of the dispatchers. At Mobile Parcel Carriers the bicycle messengers took this history seriously. Mobile Parcel Carriers' owners and dispatchers do not play games with their contract messenger services.

The industry standard in New York City is that a messenger job in the Manhattan business district (which consists of all zones from Battery Park to 125th Street in Harlem, about 10 miles in distance) has to be picked up and delivered within one hour. A rush delivery requires pickup and delivery within 45 minutes, or less than a hour. Customers pay the messenger service a flat rate for a pickup and an additional fee for each zone that is crossed to make the delivery. If a messenger job need to be delivered in a rush, there is another fee on top of the flat rate and any zone charges. Whether by bicycle, foot or van driver messenger service, the expected delivery time is the same.

At Mobile Parcel Carriers, the owners and dispatchers really took this fast time service to heart, and they instilled this view in all of their messengers. So at Mobile Parcel Carriers the bicycle messengers were the leaders in making sure the pickups and deliveries (that were not van or truck deliveries) were done on time, every time, and in all kinds of weather conditions. For their work, some of bicycle messengers earned commissions of $600.00 to $1,000.00 a week when I began working there in the spring of 2002, while foot messengers could earn $300.00 to $700.00 a week (van and truck drivers could earn $600.00 to $1,500 a week), all of them as independent contractors for Mobile Parcel Carriers. I had always wanted to be a foot messenger, and when I started at Mobile Parcel Carriers I had been a foot messenger for over 6 years already. I never had the inclination to be a bicycle messenger regardless of the higher commission pay.

At first, learning the language of the Mobile Parcel Carriers dispatchers was tough and uncomfortable. There wasn't much room to make mistakes or not listen clearly. Messenger jobs were dispatched in seconds. To receive my messenger job assignments from dispatch I used my cell phone and pay telephones. In New York City there are thousands of pay telephones all over the city. Just about every block in Manhattan has a pay telephone on it. Many of the bicycle messengers at Mobile Parcel Carriers would rent radios from the company, but most of the foot messengers had their own cell phone or used pay telephones like me. The pay telephones in Manhattan cost .25 cent per 3 minutes. Your telephone or radio at Mobile Parcel Carriers or any messenger service in New York City was your lifeline. It could determine the success or failure of your messenger business. At Mobile Parcel Carriers the control of your telephone expense is even more important because you are not reimbursed by company; the cost would actually be deducted from your earned commission income.

At every messenger service I worked for I was considered the fastest foot messenger in the office—but at Mobile Parcel Carriers the bicycle messengers were legends and they tended to look down on foot messengers. As a fast foot messenger at Mobile Parcel Carriers, I stood out in the dispatch office, because most of the foot messengers weren't as fast as bicycle messengers. Photographers and television producers would come to Mobile Parcel Carriers to find New York City's fastest bicycle messengers. Many of the foot messengers at Mobile Parcel Carriers didn't even carry messenger bags.

But as I learned more about Mobile Parcel Carriers' history, it was not about bicycle messengers, foot messengers or van and truck driving messengers. It was about doing what the customers wanted. The only stipulation at Mobile Parcel Carriers for all of their messengers was that the job be completed on time. So after I proved myself to the dispatchers and owners at Mobile Parcel Carriers that I was a fast messenger, regardless of me being on foot instead of on a bicycle, I would receive choice runs that paid high commissions for the messenger.

By my second year at Mobile Parcel Carriers, and my eighth year overall as a messenger, I was really becoming a professional courier and found myself hanging out with the elite bicycle messengers in the city. My efficiency and speed came from my track star experience and being an expert on riding the subway anywhere in the city. I memorized the Manhattan business district streets from Wall Street to Harlem, and I knew all subway routes going north, south, east and west throughout the city. Mobile Parcel Carriers identified their foot messengers who knew the subway system as "Metro Couriers". My courier code at Mobile Parcel Carriers was 300 Book. The number was just a random number they assigned to all their messengers; Book stood for the first 3 letters of my last name (Boone) and first letter of my first name (Kurt).

So by my second year at Mobile Parcel Carriers I was becoming their fastest metro courier and foot messenger, and the dispatchers and owners would regularly send me on long runs via subway. Along with my speed and knowledge of the streets, I was an expert in routing and timing, so I could complete multiple messenger jobs on time, even in difficult situations where timely pickups and deliveries was crucial. In addition to being a top messenger at Mobile Parcel Carriers, I was spending time in the bicycle messenger community, listening to the poor conditions bicycle messengers where working in. The New York Bicycle Messenger Association was an organization that was trying to unify bicycle messengers. I would go to some of their meetings and help out where I could, as well as getting to know their members at their events and parties.

After three years at Mobile Parcel Carriers I was getting tired of messenger work. I was 45 years old and still single. I didn't know where the messenger world was taking me. I had a degree in business administration from Los Angeles City College and had always wanted to be a business executive, not a career New York City Messenger, even as a "Metro Courier". My many entrepreneurial projects weren't bringing in enough cash for me to live on; they didn't pay my rent and bills, much less provide enough money for me to try to raise a family. Lorna Ware, my friend in Chicago, had ended our friendship in 2001. I wanted us to think about getting married, but she wasn't hearing that.

As a professional courier at Mobile Parcel Carriers, every day was a unique experience. As a Mobile Metro Courier specialist, I didn't know where dispatch would route me each day. I could come in one day and be in The Bronx, Manhattan and Brooklyn making pickups and deliveries. The following day I could be in Manhattan and Queens. Then on another day I could be in Washington Heights, Columbus Circle, Greenwich Village, on Wall Street and in Brooklyn, all within 7 to 8 hours time. My street and subway knowledge made me extremely fast to be able to complete jobs like that all in one day. To keep track of my messenger history, I logged the last 6 years of messenger jobs I completed in the city.

At Mobile Parcel Carriers, I grossed over $120,000 in commissionable messenger jobs with an income of around $65,000 over the four and a half years I worked there. These days I am working on trademarking my brands, Messenger 841 and Kurt Boone Authentic New York, having made some sales agreements with Wildwood Productions, TYCA Corporation and MTA. I believe that not becoming the corporate executive I dreamt about isn't a failure, but instead a greater opportunity to be a legendary New York City Messenger and entrepreneur.

At Mobile Parcel Carriers, I have done critical document pickups and deliveries for Ralph Lauren Footwear, Ralph Rucci, Walter Cronkite, Missoni, Canal Productions, Paramount Group, former President of United States Bill Clinton, Alvin Ailey, Jazz At Lincoln Center, and some of most richest addresses in the world like 10 Gracie

Square, The River House, 740 Park Avenue and The Dakota to name just a few. My spirits were high at Mobile Parcel Carriers as I went into my 5th year with the company, and 12th year overall as an elite New York City Messenger.

In the beginning of 2007, still restless from 11 year as a messenger, I was knee deep into messenger culture. Doing photo shoots, trying to find sponsors for me and other messenger events I help out on, writing a lot of poems and just documenting everything I touch in the messenger world. The bicycle messenger was still intriguing to me. Messenger bag companies where appearing everywhere. Even the major fashion houses like Prada and Calvin Klein develop designer messenger bags. But my underlining question to messenger community and bicycle messengers themselves is how do we cash in on this worldwide craze of having a messenger bag.

In the meantime, from one of my photo shoots, I wanted to do a short book about being a foot messenger and riding the subway in New York City. One day I was reading the Gotham Gazette, an on-line newsletter about current events in New York City. The Gotham Gazette was established after the September 11 tragedy to list the top stories of the city from various media outlets. From the Gotham Gazette I read a story about a photographer who was photographing people who travel through Grand Central Terminal on their commute into the city. So I contacted John Sarsgard, the photographer, about the idea I had to write an essay about my work at Grand Central Terminal as a messenger. I often used Grand Central Terminal as my central hub to get around the city fast as a foot messenger.

After speaking with John Sarsgard, he agree to do a photo shoot with me to accompany my essay. From the photos by John Sarsgard, I self-published the book "Inside Grand Central Terminal," the first messenger-based story that I had published. At Mobile Messenger Service I was still earning $300.00 to $450.00 a week base on the amount of hours I put in and deliveries I completed. My consulting business kept me in my home office most early mornings. I also help take care of my parents as my father was sick with Alzheimers disease and my mother was also elderly. Both my parents were in their 80's in 2007. Out of my other brothers and a sister, I was the only one still living in our family house to care for our parents.

After finishing "Inside Grand Central Terminal", I convinced three bicycle messengers—Amy Bolger, Kevin Bolger and Greg Ugalde—to partner in producing a book on Alleycat racing using Amy Bolger's archive of racing photos, and drawings by Greg Ugalde. I always loved Amy's photographs and Greg's illustrations. The book would be entitled "New York Alleycats".

In the process of making "New York Alleycats", Jonathan Neese, AKA "Bronx Jon", a beloved figure in the New York City Alleycat scene and a Mobile Messenger co-worker, got hit by a car one night and died a day or two later. Amy dedicated the book to "Bronx Jon".

We had a launch party for "New York Alleycats" at the pre-party and registration for "Monster Track" a big Alleycat race that bicycle messengers and street bicycle riders come to from different cities and even various countries around the world. We sold over 100 books at the "New York Alleycats" launch party.

I felt so special that Amy, Kevin and Greg trusted me with their work. I will always be indebted to them for that. Even though the "New York Alleycats" book cost roughly $2,000 to produce between the four of us, we immediately made our money back and sold out all of the 250 books we first ordered. We would go on to print more "New York Alleycats" books. But we also accomplished our mission that we wanted to establish that as messengers, we could work together and be successful business partners.

In mid-2007 I started thinking about doing something with the poetry I had written on the trains during my years of messenger work. So I started putting together a manuscript entitled "On The Subway: poetry by Kurt Boone". From the start of putting the poems together for "On The Subway", magical things started happening to me, like meeting Timothy Goodman, a young graphic designer student at the School of Visual Arts, who was already doing highly professional graphic design work even though he was still in college.

I met Timothy Goodman at Kevin Powell's book signing and reading at the Jackson McNally Bookstore in Soho, NYC. Kevin Powell is a contemporary of my generation of African-American poets. At that reading, Kevin Powell introduced Timothy Goodman as person who did his book cover. I thought Kevin Powell's book cover was hot and introduced myself to Timothy at the event, where we exchanged contact information. Later I would ask Timothy to do the book cover for "On The Subway". From the moment Timothy Goodman finished the book cover, the book had a life of its own. I would e-mail the media, booksellers and anyone who I though would be interested in reading poetry from a messenger. From that cover image I got a *New York Daily News* feature story, the opportunity to use the official subway map of MTA, a job to write a television episode for MTA News, a Barnes & Noble book signing, and producing a documentary film project entitled "Messenger Poet" by Alan Lebow Productions.

In October 2007 I started feeling a little uncomfortable. I didn't know what it was. Doing the high-speed messenger runs I wasn't feeling my usual comfortable self after a run or when I finished work for the day. I was noticing sluggishness even more when I was dispatched to be a helper for drivers who needed assistance in completing a job. Helper runs where always good runs when you got them. They paid $30.00/hr plus tips sometimes. You never know when a helper run is going to be dispatched to you. You just have to be ready when it happens. Some of the drivers I worked with at Mobile were Tunde from Nigeria, Sunni from Senegal, Sam from Nigeria, Victor and other drivers, mostly from the continent of Africa. The actual work involve in being a helper is to assist the driver carrying more than a one-man load. Generally loads consist of multiple boxes, large furniture &

large paintings. A perk of the job is you get the opportunity to deliver to some of the most expensive real estate in the city from high-rise condos to large houses in the tri-state area.

On the day after Christmas in 2007, I got up to go to work. And all of a sudden, I felt pain in my stomach and I could not move. I thought I was tired from not taking a vacation in many years. So I stayed home that day and did not go into Mobile Messenger Service to work. The next day I felt the same way. So my brother Frederick Boone came over to the house and took me to the emergency room at Franklin General Hospital in Hempstead, Long Island. Dr. Paula Young was assigned to me. I told Dr. Young I had pain in my stomach and that it was causing me not to move. Dr. Young kept me in the Emergency Room for about two days. Dr. Young had a series of tests run on me to find out what was wrong with me. Eventually I was moved to a hospital room on the third day. In the hospital room the tests continued while I was given painkillers to ease the pain. After about 5 days of testing, Dr. Young Indicated I had a blood infection and a case of pneumonia. I didn't know much about the blood infection, but I heard horror story about pneumonia that if not treated in time it could kill you.

After the diagnosis by Dr. Young I was assigned specialists for each symptom. I had a doctor for my lungs where the blood infection was found and Dr. Peter Chang for surgery. By now I had been in the hospital for over a week, and the three-doctor team hinted I might need surgery to keep the blood infection from spreading further into my lungs. Dr. Young and the lung doctor questioned me about the environment I worked in and my diet. I indicated that I worked in New York City as a foot messenger and I was exposed to September 11/World Trade Center debris on occasions. But mostly I had been exposed to all the elements in the air working outdoors in New York City for last seven years. On the diet issue, I totally failed myself. I was someone who had always tried to eat healthy, but from 2000 when I started doing messenger work again to continue funding my entrepreneurial ventures, I failed my health and did not eat right. I rarely ate fruit and virtually never took enough Vitamin C for years.

The lung doctor said that could have cause the blood infection to set in, because the immune system that protected my body from infections was weak, and it was made worse by inhaling the street elements of New York City everyday for 7 years straight. In those 7 years I never visited a doctor for any reason. Going into the second week in the hospital, it was becoming apparent I would need surgery to cut out the blood infection on my lungs. As for the pneumonia, I was receiving pills to take. In addition to the pills, I was getting medicine through IV to help fight the blood infection.

In my hospital room I had a telephone and television. My family would come visit me regularly, so I wasn't lonely. I had no health insurance and was assigned Kadija Greaves, a case worker at Franklin General Hospital. Kadija Greaves would save me from paying a very large medical bill that would eventually reach over $100,000. At about the end of the second week, the doctors confirmed I would need surgery to cut out the blood infection that was very close to entering my lungs.

While I was in the hospital, I called all my clients that I had business with to inform them of my condition, as well as my bicycle messenger friends. On the third week, the doctors prepared a contract for me to sign to OK the surgery. Dr. Chang, my surgeon, wanted me not to worry and assured me that all his surgeries were mostly successful. My surgery was very successful and the pneumonia symptoms were treated and gone. I would spend another 13 more days in the hospital for total of 27 days. My hospital bill came up to over $100,000. Through the help of my social worker to get me Medicaid and a grant from Franklin General Hospital most of my medical bill was paid. Truly God had blessed me with help. The only bill I still owe is Dr. Chang's surgery bill.

Back home at the end of January, I would rest roughly another two weeks before going back to messenger work and publishing my second poetry book, "On The Subway". Upon entering the hospital, "On The Subway" was still in the design phase at Fastback Creative Books. *The New York Daily News* Feature story came out in November.

Going back to work at Mobile Messenger Service was difficult for me, because at that point I realized I would never be back to full messenger speed for me again. When I say full messenger speed, for me that is walking 8 to 10 miles a day doing messenger pickups and deliveries, at one of the fastest foot messenger paces in the city. A Manhattan mile is about 20 short blocks, and I used to be able to walk a city mile extremely fast, in only about 6 minutes in 1990 . . . but after my hospitalization and lung surgery, in 2007 I could only do a mile in 12 minutes. Even so, both 6 minutes a mile and 12 minutes a mile would result in pickup and delivery times that could earn me more commission on foot than your average bicycle messenger.

Eventually, around May of 2008, I asked my cousin Stephanie Wilson to loan me $200.00 to release "On The Subway". I also knew poetry wasn't selling well in bookstores and in the general marketplace with many book distributors outright declining to sell poetry books. As a poet I couldn't give in to this market circumstance. Facing this difficulty as I wrote my poetry and essays, I started to direct my attention to filmmakers. In 2007 I started outlining "Asphalt Warrior", a memoir of my life as a messenger, and completed a few chapters. So after "On The Subway" was released, I asked Sarah Mishkin and Oliver Werner of Fastback Creative Books to do a graphic sketch for the book cover of "Asphalt Warrior", so I could send it around to book publishers, the media and filmmakers.

In my research to find filmmakers I came across a website called reel-exchange.com. Reel-exchange.com had a database of the addresses for various filmmakers, editors and producers to exchange ideas and to submit potential film projects. I picked out five film directors from the Reel-exchange.com database and sent them a pdf of the "Asphalt Warrior" bookcover, in the hopes that they would consider making a film based on the book. Out of the five filmmakers, all of them express great interest in my messenger story. Most of them wanted money from me to make the film except two. Out of the two who expressed interest in my story without money upfront, I picked Studio 108 out of Richmond, VA. Jack Hartmann, one of the film directors at Studio 108, liked my messenger story a lot, but was very interested in doing the film if it was not just about me but about the whole messenger world, inspired from my memoir "Asphalt Warrior".

By 2008 I had been a foot messenger for 12 years. I had received product sponsorship from Timbuk 2 and Manhattan Portage... began two clothing lines, Messenger 841 and Kurt Boone Authentic New York... developed business opportunities with clothing manufacturers and distributors including Wildwood Productions, TYCA, Vision Embroidery and Kiat USA dba Metro Merchandise . . . and in November of 2008 I wrote a poem for MTA Transit News Holiday Show, where transit workers read a different line that was video recorded and broadcast on a community television channel in New York City. It was my first writing to be adapted to a film.

I also had an agreement with Jack Hartmann to use my upcoming book "Asphalt Warrior" as the basis for a film on the messenger world. We both came up with working titles. I thought the film should be called "Courier Streets" and Studio 108 wanted to call the film "Move".

Through my membership in DV Republic I had the opportunity to pitch HBO Documentary the film project "Courier Streets" with an under-3-minutes clip about the project. So I sent some photos and a one-hour video interview about my life as a messenger, which I had done with Noreen Mallory, a freelance journalist, and Carl Weston of Videograf Productions. Studio 108 took my photos and video and came up with a 90-second trailer on "Courier Streets". Jacqueline Glover of HBO liked the trailer and wanted to see more.

Unfortunately Jack Hartmann sustained an injury playing a sport that threw the project off track. So the beginning of 2009 wasn't looking too good. I was still tired of messenger work and would have quit in a second if the right opportunity came my way. During the whole year of 2008 messenger jobs were declining and my paychecks where getting smaller every week. There was a global recession going on and it definitely affected me.

My father died in January of 2009, he was 85 years old.

Messenger work at Mobile Messenger Service took a serious decline in January 2009. There were not that many companies calling in messenger jobs. The American recession was really happening. I was used to seeing vacant stores downtown in the area that was had been affected by the tragic events of September 11—but now I was seeing vacant storefronts all around the business districts of Manhattan. Nothing was more shocking than seeing vacant storefronts on Manhattan's super-rich upper eastside. The upper eastside is a retail market supported by the people living in million-dollar apartments, of which 740 Park Avenue, 10 Gracie Square and The River House were some of most exclusive real estate holdings in the world. (I think I mentioned that as a Mobile messenger I made deliveries to all three 3 addresses.)

It was shocking to me, picking up and delivering messenger jobs on the upper eastside, and almost every corner I turned there was another vacant store front. The recession was scary to me, fearing I might not have a job soon—even though working as a messenger for 13 years I had never been scared of anything. Back at Mobile Messenger Service there were layoffs of the back-office staff. Staff workers who had worked at Mobile many more years than me were laid off. Chet, Richard, Jim and Walter, all hard workers at Mobile, were let go, though Chet and Walter went back to work as commission foot messengers. My fellow bicycle messengers would come to work ready to go and be left with just one or two runs for the whole day. Butch 2 of FTP Graffiti Crew and a mobile bicycle messenger moved to Texas, and Stewart, another bicycle messenger, moved back to Florida.

I asked my mother to lower my room rent from $600.00 a month to $400.00 a month because of the national recession. But my mother at the time was also starting to feel ill; she was 83 years old, and my rent became secondary in importance to my helping her and taking good care of the house, especially after the loss of my father in January of 2009.

In February 2009, *The New York Times* called me and said they wanted to do a feature story on a foot messenger. The story in *The New York Times* was a great piece and every one of my friends, co-workers and relatives who read it loved it.

Prior to *The New York Times* article, I had contacted Seagull Bags after a Cranksgiving event in 2008 and let them know I wanted to make a signature bag in my name (opposite). Seagull Bags agreed to make a limited edition of 25 bags with my Kurt Boone Signature logo drawn by Greg Ugalde, New York City's premier messenger street artist. The messenger bags would be released in May of 2009. In March of 2009, Ian Dowden of Chicken Switch, a boutique action sport agency, got Converse Sneakers to provide me with product.

Then over the summer, Function Drinks, a manufacturer and distributor of beverages, provided me with 2 cases to drink on my messenger jobs. Function Drinks is known for their brands "Urban Detox" and "Alternative Energy" (page 64). I met Function Drinks in 2008 at the Fancy Food Tradeshow in New York when I was doing market research for H.K. Farm, my cousin Handy Kennedy's family farm in Georgia. H.K. Farm has been family-owned since 1869.

The "Courier Streets" film production project slowed up, so I de-cided to submit "On The Subway" for a film project to the directors listed on reel-exchange.com. Alan Lebow of ALP Digital liked the storyline, and we met to discuss working together on a film using my poetry. In the summer of 2009, ALP Digital began shooting "Mes-senger Poet", a series of short films based on my poetry about life in the city and about life as a New York City messenger.

As my stature as a foot messenger in New York City became further documented, Carl Weston, an ex-coworker of mine at Mobile Mes-senger Service, had interest in doing a documentary film on me about me being a foot messenger in the city. In 2009 we began shooting "The Foot Messenger", a Carl Weston Production.

My beloved mother died on Thanksgiving Night, November 26, 2009. She will be greatly missed by me, my brothers, my sister and the entire Boone family.

I got back to work at Mobile on November 30 thinking about all the great things I had achieved as a foot messenger in New York City, but I wanted to continue my dream to be a great writer and entrepreneur. I had also managed to complete my first audio book in 2009. Barbara Groark of Groark Audio read "On The Subway" and offered me an audio book contract to publish the audio book on audible.com.

In 2010 I don't know what to expect as a New York City messenger but I am ready for all the success it may bring me. What follows are a few tales of messenger life in the city.

"THE RUSH FOR DR. KONALDI"

I called Mobile Messenger dispatch from my cell phone from a public space bench between skyscrapers at 53rd and 54th Street. Forest at Mobile Messenger dispatch gave me a rush job for Dr. Konaldi. The pick up was at 525 East 68th Street and the delivery was at 177 Fort Washington Avenue. 525 East 68th Street was New York Hospital and 177 Fort Washington Avenue was Columbia Presbyterian Hospital, where Dr. Konaldi was located. To begin working on the job, I walked fast down a few blocks over to 55th Street subway station and hopped on R train for two stops to Lexington Avenue, where I then transferred to the 6 train at 59th Street and Lexington Avenue for 1 stop to 68th Street and Lexington.

From 68th Street and Lexington Avenue, I walked really fast, almost like a light run, about a half mile down 68th Street to New York Hospital at the 525 East 68th Street address. At New York Hospital I was a little confused on which Hospital wing to go to, since there are many wings in New York Hospital. After getting on a few elevators trying to get to room 433, I found that none of the elevators would go to fourth floor, so I finally asked someone at the information desk in the lobby. The information desk told me to take K wing elevators to the fourth floor. After taking the K wing elevators I finally arrived at room 433 for the pick up, which were a bunch of CD's for Jane.

By this time 45 minutes was off the clock; I got the job dispatched to me at 1:45pm and it was now 2:30pm. To go to 177 Fort Washington Avenue, I would walk really fast, again a little over a half mile, from 68th Street to 79th Street on First Avenue. At First Avenue and 79th Street I hopped on the M79 crosstown bus from the Eastside to Westside, getting off at Central Park West and 81st street, where I caught the C train at the 81st street station, riding it up to 168th Street and Broadway. At the 168th Street station, I walked real fast up the stairs to exit on the street at 168th street. I again picked up the pace and walked fast, down 1 block to 177 Fort Washington Avenue, where Dr. Konaldi's office in Presbyterian Hospital is located. I entered the lobby, then showed the security guard my Mobile Messenger ID card so that I could get a pass to go Dr. Konaldi's office reception area on the 2nd floor to make my delivery. I delivered the CDs in a pretty fast time, which was just a few minutes over 90 minutes.

MARY HOWARD STUDIO: OCTOBER 10, 2010

Rainy days are always the hardest for me. This rainy day the wind was blowing slightly and the rain was steady. I called Mobile Dispatch from 53rd Street and Lexington Avenue. Cuz (that's his nickname) was the dispatcher, and he gave me a rush pickup at Mary Howard Studio in Brooklyn. The "rush" designation meant I had to get to Brooklyn as fast as I could to make the pickup and rush back to Manhattan for the delivery. So I got on the E train towards the World Trade Center at 53rd Street and Lexington Avenue and took it to

West 4th street, where I transferred to the F train to Coney Island, even though dispatch told me to take the F train to Carroll Street. Something in my mind said I was going to slowly, as if there was a quicker route I wasn't aware of.

So I got off the F train at Carroll street. The rain was still coming down and the wind continued to blow. I was walking as fast as I could with my umbrella through the rain and wind to get to Mary Howard Studio. Mary Howard Studio was about a half mile from the Carroll Street train station. Not knowing what the package was that I was going to pick up, I feared it was going to be an oversize package that would be difficult to carry in the rain, and if it were oversize it might get wet in spite of the umbrella I was using, and would also cause me to be very slow.

When I got to Mary Howard Studio the rain and wind continued to hit my body. My fears were realized when the package I received was an oversize box in a shopping bag. However, even though it was oversize it was still manageable, so I put it in a large black plastic bag to help protect it from the rain. As I was leaving Mary Howard Studio an employee came out of the office and yelled at me, saying "Where are you going?" I said I was going to get the F train where I had come from. She then indicated to me that the F train was the slow way to get to Manhattan. She told me to take the train around the corner, Union Street Station, where I could catch the R train to Manhattan. She further indicated that she informed the Mobile dispatch operators prior to my pick up that the F train was the slow way to go, and that she would called Mobile dispatch again to tell them not to send messengers by the F train line. Finally she reminded me that the messenger job was a rush delivery and asked me if Mobile dispatch told me that and I said yes.

Now all this dialogue took place between me and the client in the rain, and lasted just about 2 minutes or less. However, because of the emotion of this messenger job, it felt like much more time was involved. Still tense from knowing how important this rush job was, I got around the corner as fast I could. I was hoping the R train would arrive quickly at the Union Street station. The R took 15 minutes to arrive, taking more time off the clock. But I kept a clear mind and continued to work as hard as I could, hoping that the train would move fast. For sure I am being timed by the dispatcher for how long it took from the initial call to my call-in at the delivery destination. It's a pressure I relish . . . and dread if the delivery time was too slow.

The delivery point for Mary Howard Studio was a set designing firm at Pier 59, Stage C at the Hudson River and 18th Street. The R train took me to 14th Street and Union Square where I transferred to L train to 8th Avenue and 14th Street. Pier 59 is actually on 18th Street and 11th Avenue. From 14th Street I would continue to walk fast as possible, because the job was a rush delivery to 18th Street and 11th Avenue in the rain and wind. Arriving at Stage C with the delivery, the Stage C receptionist seemed happy their package had arrived. In return I was very happy for doing a good job.

"CITY TIDBITS"

Some of the many places I get to see as a foot messenger are public spaces all over Manhattan, many of them unknown to tourists or even native New Yorkers. These public spaces I have visited through my work experience as a messenger are throughout Manhattan, from Battery Park City to 125th Street. Battery Park City, located in downtown Manhattan, is easy to get to on foot; it is walking distance from the 4 and 5 train station at Bowling Green or the R train station at Whitehall Street. Battery Park City is full of beautiful public spaces with benches, green grass, manicured trees, sculptures, a waterfront esplanade, walking paths and bicycle lanes. Since I am a poet, one of my favorite downtown places is the newly built Poet House on 10 River Terrace, where you can browse poetry books for free or listen to a poetry reading on tape. On the east side of Manhattan, there are parks, walkways and bike lanes that run along FDR Drive all the way from 125th Street to the Chinatown area at the downtown end of the island.

In the Times Square area, there are several small public spaces with public benches and restaurants. These are located in the middle of blocks, sandwiched in between towering skyscrapers, from 54th Street to 47th Street, between Broadway and Fifth Avenue. There is a new beautiful walkway at the Henry Miller Theatre which is next door to Conde Nast Headquarters, located in the middle of 42nd Street and 43rd Street, between 6th Avenue and Broadway.

In the Lincoln Center area, between 59th Street and 66th Street on Broadway and Columbus Avenue, there are beautiful public spaces with benches all around. The Lincoln Center Atrium also has tables and food vendors. At the Lincoln Center Atrium they have public events all year long and free Wi Fi. You can get to Lincoln Center by taking 1, D, B, C and A trains to 59th Street and Columbus Circle. The Jazz Museum at Lincoln Center is also a great place to visit and sit down in the public space. The view of the city is great from up there.

A lot of the bicycle messengers ride along the west side bicycle lanes to take their packages downtown. But if you like riding a bicycle, you can go from 125th Street to Battery Park City on your bicycle getting a cool breeze from the Atlantic Ocean as you ride right down next to the West Side Highway.

At 53rd Street between Madison Avenue and Fifth Avenue there is a beautiful public space with benches and an art installation. A few more blocks down Fifth Avenue at Trump Tower, there is a public atrium on 57th Street, another place to hang out in the city if you have free time. Trump Tower is also right across the street from the Sony atrium that has food vendors and seats inside.

Uptown at 94th Street between Madison Avenue and Park Avenue there is a public space area alongside of a private apartment building. And finally on the upper eastside from 59th Street to 93rd Street between East End Avenue and Fifth Avenue there are many well-kept public spaces attached or next door to private apartment buildings. Often you will see older people relaxing on the benches in the sunshine, or younger people talking together, or on their cell phones, or nannies or young mothers sitting down with their strollers to take a break. These public spaces are great places to sit down and relax in a city where everybody is in a rush to get somewhere, including me, the messenger.

"SUBWAY STORIES"

As a foot messenger and mail runner I have seen many kinds of people and characters riding the subway all over New York City's five boroughs. Some of the characters I have seen I will try to describe as best I can in this section.

There was the no-legged beggar with a tin can, riding a skateboard. The man would push his skateboard through the subway cars transfer doors that allow you to move between subway cars. He would announce to all passengers in the subway car that he was begging for money by banging his tin can on the train car floors. It was something to see a legless man on a skateboard begging for money on the train. I ran into him off and on for years.

Another character was a disabled Puerto Rican in a wheelchair, with the Puerto Rican flag attached to the wheelchair, being pushed by an associate asking for money in the subway car. I would see this Puerto Rican beggar on the train for many years.

A big black man with a Muslim outfit would get on the E train that I took to worked everyday. When I say big, I mean someone 6'8" tall; his head would nearly bump into the ceiling of the train cars. He would carry a large bag with sandwiches for the homeless. His motto

was: you could be homeless too. "Some of you are one paycheck away from being homeless," he would tell all the passengers in the train car. I don't know what compelled this guy to speak to subway riders like that, but he did for a couple of years I ran into him.

There was this African-American woman who I would see all around the city on different trains, asking for money for the homeless. I don't know if she was running a scam, but I saw her for years on the subway.

A bum sat next to me for 25 minutes going into Manhattan on the E train. It was a blessing he didn't smell. The bums that smell make people get out of their seat and clear out of the subway car, but some riders stay in the car no matter what a bum smell like. 100% of the time I would move to the next car to avoid the smell from a subway bum.

The Mexicans performers are another group of characters. The Mexican performers who dress in authentic Mexican apparel with Sombreros on their heads. They would sing songs in Spanish then pass around there Sombrero for donations. What got me was the Mexican outfits look expensive, yet they were begging for money on the train, which is technically a crime.

Another beggar on train I would see quite often was a blind man and his seeing-eye dog. This blind man had a tape recorder that hung from his body that played music very loud. The blind man also carried a newspaper article that had his picture and a story about him panhandling for money on the train. He would walk back and forth on the subway car with a plastic bucket, seeking money. I saw this blind man for many years on the E train going to work.

Break dancing kids are another popular begging group of characters I would run into riding the subway all over New York City doing messenger work. These young people and sometimes children would do actual break dancing moves on a moving subway car. One day a kid did a flip on the train and almost hit me in the mouth. If that would have happened, I know I would have had many broken teeth and possibly a broken jaw. I fell from the force of that flip. It was a scary moment for me.

Then there are group of black men who I call Doo-Wop singers because they sing classic doo-wop songs. Through the years I have seen different groups of black men doing the same routine. These men sang pretty well. During the holiday season these middle-aged men would sing classic songs like "Rudolf Red-Nosed Reindeer" and "Jingle Bells". They are African-American men who seem to be in their 60s and look like fathers, grandfathers and uncles. I felt these guys were disturbed for holding a brown paper bag out for money while singing classic doo-wop songs.

Then last but not least that I can recall are the official subway musicians who sing or play instruments, seeking donations for their performances, who are sanctioned by the MTA. You could usually tell the official subway musicians because most of them would put out the official subway banner wherever they where performing, making sure subway riders knew they were MTA official subway musicians. There are three subway musicians that stand out in my memory riding the subway all over New York City. There was a family of horn players from Chicago who play very good jazz music, with slick hip-hop tones along with the harmony of a college marching band. The band had at least 7 members. Another official subway musician I saw a lot was the Saw Lady who play music with her saw. Finally the Black Hillbillies were pretty good and their hillbilly outfits were cool too.

Skyscrapers, Doormen and 9/11

GROWING UP IN NEW YORK CITY, AT TIMES YOU CAN TAKE the skyscrapers—that line Madison Avenue, Fifth Avenue, Park Avenue and Wall Street—for granted. As an African-American youth from a middle-class family, I dreamed about what it would be like working in skyscrapers, especially the famous ones like the Empire State Building, The World Trade Center and the Woolworth Building. Then I dreamed about what it would be like to be rich and shopping on Fifth Avenue or Madison Avenue, and living on Park Avenue. These buildings and streets were world-famous.

In my youth, not only was I a track star, I was learning the streets of Manhattan in my free time. As it was for me, my friends and other youth from all over the city could use our street knowledge to be messengers.

But getting back to obtaining the American Dream and achieving the success that could have me living on Park Avenue—well, it was starting to be a difficult vision to achieve. I grew up in Cambria Heights and went to Junior High School 192 in Hollis, Queens, where I began to be offered drugs to take and the opportunity to be in a gang when I was just around 13 or 14 years old. So in my mind what was happening in my neighborhood made obtaining the American Dream blurry, because of the drugs and gang activities that surrounded me.

On top of that, the stories I heard from my parents, and reading history books about the African-American experience in America, all made it seem that obtaining the American Dream would not be a cakewalk. Nevertheless, I wanted to work in those skyscrapers and be rich enough to live on Park Avenue. How or if I would get there I did not know, but I would try my hardest.

My freshman year in college I got an internship as a mailroom clerk at MGM headquarters at 729 Seventh Avenue in Times Square, my first skyscraper job. I delivered mail to all 17th floors in the building, including the chairman's office. At first it looked like a good start toward achieving my American Dream or success story, but in actuality I was dabbling in smoking marijuana, just getting passing grades in college, and trying to help in preventing the spread of youth crime and violence in my neighborhood by assisting in counseling youth crime prevention sessions.

At that time, New York City as I saw it and experienced it was in a sort of a crisis: crime was occurring rapidly all over the city, and in the heart of New York City Tourism, Times Square was full of X-rated movies houses and peep shows. So in reality I didn't know what to think, but just took everything as it happened in my life.

After finishing my internship at United Artists/MGM, I then began working full-time for a crime prevention organization for one year. After I finished that year, I wanted to get back to my dream of having a successful career in business. I joined the Navy in 1981, but didn't make it out of boot camp, so I came back to New York City. Crime was still going on around the city and many of my friends were still taking drugs.

I should say that not all my friends and peers were involved with drugs and gangs. Some of my friends obtained college scholarships and would eventually become doctors and lawyers. None of my friends and peers would obtain their success through corporate America's executive suites.

My dream that most of my family, peers and friends knew I had all my life was to be a corporate executive. Nevertheless I left New York City again for Los Angeles where I lived for the next 6 years. In Los Angeles I graduated from college and became a store manager for Radio Shack. Eventually after 6 years I moved back to New York City in 1988, where I rekindled my dream to work downtown in the skyscrapers and become a business executive.

In 1989, at 30 years of age, I became an insurance agent for MetLife in Maspeth, Queens. I was at MetLife for a little over a year and sold over 1 million dollars in life insurance premiums. In 1988 and 1989 the city was changing to try and clean up the streets, especially in the Times Square area where the X-rated movie houses and peep show were located. In 1990 I went back to work in Manhattan as a messenger for Rapid Messenger Service.

In the early 1990s I started making pickups and deliveries for the super-rich in Manhattan. When I think of super-rich, it refers to people or families who can afford to live in multi-million dollar apartments. This was my first introduction to the world of doormen, for I rarely ever delivered packages personally to super-rich people who could afford a multi-million apartment in person—I would just leave the packages with their doormen. These million-dollar apartments were on Park Avenue, Fifth Avenue, the upper Westside and upper Eastside (from 59th Street to 110th Street); this was the main area for doorman buildings.

For Rapid Messenger Service I did a lot of work for George Soros, one of the richest men in the world, whose building was on Central Park South. As I am writing this in October of 2010, I don't remember a lot of the names of the people whose packages I picked up and delivered. The names of the owners of these apartments and in some cases penthouses vary widely; some of the names of the super rich were not easy last names like Smith or Johnson, but often had more of an international flavor, like Katrina Von Heuvel the editor of The

Nation Magazine, who I work for now at Mobile Messenger Service. I have actually been to Katrina Von Heuvel apartment to make a delivery numerous times, but mostly the kids sign for the package at the door. I have never met Katrina Von Heuvel herself.

Getting back to 1990s, I also noticed the different uniforms doormen wore. Each building I went to whether on Park Avenue, Fifth Avenue, the upper Eastside or upper Westside, doormen had a unique uniform to identify that they worked for that building. Coincidentally, in my 14 years as a messenger, I can't recall ever seeing a woman doorman. In some cases doormen wore white gloves, but that was not very often in my experience.

As a messenger I also enjoy looking at the magnificent foyers of each building—even though, as a messenger you were not allowed to sit in the furniture of the lobby, even if you had to wait for a pickup. Of course, in smaller, less expensive apartment buildings, I could sit in the foyer. You can tell the people who live in these exclusive buildings were rich because of the foyer; just looking at the furniture and art on the wall alone was proof enough.

As a messenger you are slightly important, just as the doorman is, because on the other side of the pick up or delivery there is an important person expecting the pickup or the package—and that person is usually the rich person who called for the messenger. I should say that in those moments between pickup and completing the delivery, you are extremely important, but when the job is finished you mean nothing. Incidentally, most of the exclusive apartment buildings and condominiums are skyscrapers as well.

New York City is the skyscraper capital of the world. Working in the 1990s as a messenger I would make pickups and deliveries in hundreds of skyscrapers located on the famous streets of Manhattan, from the bottom of the Manhattan island at Water Street to the top of the messenger districts at 125th Street. Nothing felt better than going into a prestigious law firm, accounting firm, insurance company or

Fortune 500 company offices as a messenger. You were a priority to the receptionist, messenger center, secretary, CEO, executive, manager, owner in that company from the minute you arrive in that office. There are no surprises in the messenger business. You are there in that office for a reason, and usually an important one at that—and although messenger pay doesn't reflect that, the owner's pay of the messenger services does.

There were many messenger service companies in 1990s making millions of dollars in revenue. Foot messengers are lucky to make little above minimum wage, although bicycle messengers (something I have never done) were making good money in the 1990s. Drivers, truck drivers and motorcycle couriers were supposed to be making way more than minimum wage. I was not an owner, so I can not tell you what bicycle and driving messenger make exactly.

Below is a partial list of buildings where I have picked up or delivered packages:

SUPER-RICH APARTMENTS:
The Dakota
San Remo
10 Gracie Square
740 Park Avenue
15 CPW
The River House
One Sutton Place South

CORPORATE OFFICE BUILDINGS:
Rockefeller Center
CBS Building
GE Building
Flatiron Building

World Trade Center: Tower 1 and 2
Empire State Building
Woolworth Building
Chrysler Building
Time Life Building
Hearst Building
Pan Am Building (Now Met-Life Building)
Hearst Building
Conde Nast Building
Helmsley Building
Waldorf Astoria Hotel
The Plaza Hotel
Trump Tower
IBM Building
Sony Building

In the 1990s I also started making pickups and deliveries at the World Trade Center. At first in the 1990s going to World Trade Center was fun, taking the elevator to the sky lobby and then transferring to the sky tower elevators going all the way up to the 110th floor. I think the highest floor I made a delivery to was the 109th floor. I made a lot of pickups and deliveries in the World Trade Center, tower 1 and tower 2, prior to the first terrorist attack on the World Trade Center in 1994. As a messenger I would just go into building 1 or building 2, but I think there were seven buildings altogether that made up the World Trade Center complex. In those days, going into World Trade Center, tower 1 or tower 2, I did not need to show my ID or be checked by security. I would just go into the building and go to floor I was picking up from or delivering to.

After the first terrorist attack on World Trade Center, building security at the World Trade Center and other buildings in the city began to change. After the first terrorist attack, visitors or messengers going into tower 1 or tower 2 at the World Trade Center had to get a security clearance to go into the building. At the security checkpoint your picture was taken for use on a temporary ID card. With that temporary ID you could go into tower 1 or tower 2.

In 1995 I left the messenger industry and did not return until 2000. In 2000 as a messenger I could still pretty much go into any building without an ID, and there were very few security checkpoints that you had to pass through. This all changed radically after September 11, 2001. Over the next 9 years as a messenger, I saw the whole Manhattan business district change to having a security checkpoint at every skyscraper in Manhattan. Each year I would visit more buildings with security checkpoints installed.

Then certain buildings established separate messenger centers. These building messenger centers handled all packages being picked up or delivered to that building. Some buildings like 4 Times Square (Conde Nast Headquarters), or 300 West 57th Street (the Hearst Building) handle hundreds of messengers from different companies picking up or delivering to that building. Some of these messenger centers were elaborate, with package scanners to detect bombs, computer package tracking systems with bar code labels and scanners. In some instances if you had to go to a floor for a pickup or a delivery at a building like the Chrysler building or the Citicorp building, you had to be escorted by an authorized building messenger who had an access card to the building elevators. The building-authorized messenger escort would stay with you until you finished the pickup or delivery, and then escort you out of the building.

Over the past few years, the American recession began to affect the retail businesses of Manhattan, with many retailers closing up. I saw the decline with my own eyes, and I could hardly believe all these retail stores were shutting their doors. From big retailers like Tower Records and Virgin Megastores, down to all kinds of small businesses like the local pizza shops and mom & pop grocery stores all over

Manhattan. Many of these retailers were located in the wealthiest parts of Manhattan.

It reminded me of the Wall Street district after the events of September 11th occurred: for the first two years after the event, many retailers closed their doors. On some blocks it looked like a bomb had hit that block. Some blocks were dark with most of the retailers closed.

As far as messenger work, some days you hated to go downtown because there was no messenger work going back uptown, so that meant once you completed the messenger job downtown, the chance of dispatch giving you more work was slim. So I would ride back uptown to Grand Central Terminal or Times Square to get more messenger work. That time spent traveling back uptown was lost. Time was money to me and other messengers in the industry. In my eight years at Mobile Messenger Service I estimated I grossed over $200,000 in messenger jobs revenue.

Of course, just because there wasn't messenger work coming out of World Trade Center area, doesn't take away from the lives lost on September 11. It was a great tragedy then and is a great tragedy today. My heartfelt sympathy goes out to all the families who lost loved ones on September 11.

So in all in my 14 years plus as a messenger, I have seen my skyscraper and super-rich lifestyle experience in abundance. Is it the dream I wanted as a kid? Absolutely not, but it sure is interesting to be able to see it close-up.

Entrepreneurial Spirit

WHEN I WAS A COLLEGE STUDENT IN THE EARLY 1980s at California State University in Long Beach, I read a lot about advances in technology. I read any articles or news clips I could find on what Bill Gates of Microsoft and Steve Jobs of Apple Computers were doing in building their companies. In my junior year at Cal State Long Beach I went to the college job fair and some companies would hire you before you graduated and you could finish your degree in a night school program. I already had my AA business degree from Los Angeles City College, so I decided to leave college before graduating with a bachelor degree and take an entry-level job in corporate America. Far from my internship as a mailclerk at United Artists/MGM that I completed in 1978 in New York City, I took a job as a manager trainee at Radio Shack, The Technology Store.

The manager trainee program at Radio Shack taught you the skills to become a manager at a Radio Shack Store. So I was sent to the Costa Mesa store to learn about and how to sell Radio Shack products. Radio Shack sold consumer electronic products and sales representatives, manager trainees and managers were paid by salary, commissions and bonuses. At the Costa Mesa store I sold semi-conductors, light bulbs, radios, scanners, television sets, cell phones, telephones, circuit boards and other electronic products.

After training at the Costa Mesa store I was promoted to manager and got my own store in Fountain Valley, California. Fountain Valley is located in Orange County, a suburb of the city of Los Angeles. This was my first entrepreneurial experience. I was 27 years old and in charge of a six-figure location.

The experience was exciting and gave me the opportunity to make a name for myself as a retail manager. The first few months I was doing well with my sales, making the quota amount required of our district managers. Then after my first two months sales started declining and I wasn't making my manager sales quota. Shortly after I was fired for not meeting my sales quota.

After I got fired from Radio Shack I went to work for a temp agency. Because of the firing and other factors like paying my rent on time, buying food to eat and making car payments, living in Los Angeles on my own began to become stressful. After a two-month temp assignment at AT&T as a telemarketing representative selling Merlin telephone systems to businesses, I began to think about moving back to New York City. Following discussions with my family and running low on money, my parents sent me a ticket to come back home to New York City. I returned from Los Angeles in fall of 1988 with a fragile body and skin rashes all over my body. I began to eat a lot and went to see a dermatologist who said my skin rashes could have been cause by the stress and sun while living in Los Angeles.

At this time I wasn't thinking of being an entrepreneur. I was thinking of building a corporate career. I had my AA degree in business administration and another 40 credits from California State University, Long Beach. I started doing interviews for a career job while working at temporary agency based in Manhattan. I lucked out when I passed the insurance agent examination and got a job as insurance agent with MetLife. MetLife was cool except I felt discriminated against and brought a lawsuit against MetLife that got dismissed by the Human Rights Commission for not being a discrimination case. While

I was still at MetLife a client told me that I should think about being an entrepreneur. From MetLife I went to work for John Hancock Financial Services as an independent broker for about six months. When I failed at that I became a delivery driver for Domino Pizza. I was thirty years old.

Then on Christmas Day in 1989 I got into car accident while driving in my Cambria Heights community. The accident totaled my car, but I and the passengers in the other car came out okay. Since my car was totaled, I rented a car and continue to work for Domino Pizza—but after the car accident I started seriously thinking about being an entrepreneur.

With that said, I decided to go back to messenger work, with the intent to become an entrepreneur. I had a AA degree in business and marketing experience with Fortune 500 companies including Tandy Corporation (Radio Shack), AT&T, MetLife, and John Hancock Financial Services, plus various other jobs in Corporate America with MGM/UA, Vons Grocery Company, and Domino Pizza.

I responded to an advertisement in the *New York Post* for commission messengers and I got hired at Rapid Messenger Service immediately. While I was working at Rapid Messenger Service, I started looking for projects where I could use my corporate marketing experience and develop entrepreneurial projects.

I joined the Black Filmmaker Foundation, because I saw that black filmmakers and actors like Spike Lee, Denzel Washington, Warrington Hudlin, Eddie Murphy and others where becoming quite successful in Hollywood. The Black Filmmaker Foundation presented opportunities in Hollywood for African-Americans through lectures and events. I got some head shots made of me and volunteered at the Black Filmmaker Foundation office. Eventually this would lead to an extra position in Spike Lee's epic film "Malcolm X" starring Denzel Washington. My extra job was to sit next to Angela Bassett in the assassination scene of "Malcolm X" played by Denzel Washington.

Since acting wasn't my best opportunity, I started looking for other opportunities to apply my marketing skills. I love African-American books and soon an opportunity would come to get involved with Quarterly Black Review of Books through the New York Association of Black Journalists, of which I was also a member. In 1993 I would become a part-time distribution manager for QBR. Through my work with Max Rodriguez, the publisher of QBR, I helped obtain more subscriptions and secured newsstand distribution through Tower Records, Barnes & Noble Booksellers, African-American owned bookstores and other bookstores. While still working at Rapid Messenger Service, I was also doing marketing projects for Milestone Media, a black comic book company owned by DC Comics.

Also while working at Rapid Messenger Service as a messenger, I began to establish myself as author. I began writing poetry in high school, and in college I wrote sports articles for Pandora's Box at York College and the L.A. Collegian at Los Angeles City College.

Through the Black Filmmaker Foundation I met Mike Ryals, a correction officer and one of my brother's co-workers. My brother Elliott Boone Jr. is also correction officer and a top vendor at Yankee Stadium. I mentioned to Mike Ryals that I was a poet and wanted to published an old manuscript of poetry I had from a past Yale University competition for unpublished poetry books called Yale Series of Younger Poets. I didn't win the competition but held on to manuscript. The manuscript was entitled "Looking For Myself," a collection of poems I wrote after high school about me growing up in Queens, New York.

Mike Ryals agreed to help me self-publish the book through Dorrance Publishing Company. In addition I also had completed a memoir entitle "A Kid's Dream" about my dream to be college basketball player, which was represented by the Barbara Bauer Literary Agency and Hans Management Company, a sport agent firm, for book rights. I started getting rejection notices on "A Kid's Dream", and before I

CLOCKWISE FROM TOP LEFT: With Joey Krill (photo by Michaelle Chapoteau); *Premium Rush* casting call (with Alfred Bobe, photo by Jose Morales); with Takuya Sakamoto (photo by Michaelle Chapoteau); *Premium Rush* casting call (with Felipe, photo by Jose Morales)

CLOCKWISE FROM TOP LEFT: With Tone, an organizer of Cranksgiving Alleycat (photo by Noreen Mallory); with Stone Tone (Tony, photo by Michaelle Chapoteau); *Monster Track XI* (with Victor) with Austin Horse (photo by Michaelle Chapoteau); *Premium Rush* casting call (with Ninja, Kevin Bolger, Jenessa Starks, and Jose Morales)

CLOCKWISE FROM TOP LEFT: With Jeff Hill (photo by John Sarsgard); Ian Dowden of Chicken Switch; Barnes & Noble book signing with Greg Ugalde, Amy Bolger, and Kevin Bolger (wearing cap, photo by Bob Gore); Chris Thormann (photo by Michaelle Chapoteau); with Roland of Reload Bags

CLOCKWISE FROM TOP LEFT:
At Mobile Messenger Service's dispatch office (photo by John Sarsgard); with Carlos Ramirez of Cyclehawk Messengers; with Jackie Zappala of Chrome Industries at the launch party for their New York City store (photo by Jose Morales); with Michaelle Chapoteau (photo by Annette E. Brown); with Kim Perfetto, bicycle messenger and professional trainer

CLOCKWISE FROM TOP LEFT: With Jay, a Mobile Messenger co-worker; Kenton Hoppas, bicycle messenger and director of the film *Career Courier* which I have a scene in; with Heather Mueller, bicycle messenger and two-time "Monster Track" Alleycat race winner; with Greg Ugalde, *Messenger Poet* illustrator; Enrico Fales, co-worker and veteran foot messenger; *Premium Rush* casting call (with Ninja, Hiromi and Hector, photo by Jose Morales); with Marshall, a veteran messenger at Mobile Messenger Service

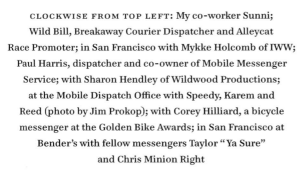

CLOCKWISE FROM TOP LEFT: My co-worker Sunni;
Wild Bill, Breakaway Courier Dispatcher and Alleycat
Race Promoter; in San Francisco with Mykke Holcomb of IWW;
Paul Harris, dispatcher and co-owner of Mobile Messenger
Service; with Sharon Hendley of Wildwood Productions;
at the Mobile Dispatch Office with Speedy, Karem and
Reed (photo by Jim Prokop); with Corey Hilliard, a bicycle
messenger at the Golden Bike Awards; in San Francisco at
Bender's with fellow messengers Taylor "Ya Sure"
and Chris Minion Right

left Rapid Messenger Service, I decided to put the manuscript away until I found a better opportunity to publish the book.

Still doing messenger work at Rapid Messenger Service while also doing freelance marketing work at Shade Magazine, I got an opportunity to work for Avon Products. I knew little about Avon Products except my mother bought it from our next door neighbor, Mrs. Torrence, and my father used Avon cologne and musk. Avon Products were hiring independent sales representatives in my district of Jamaica, New York. Mary Poinson was the district manager who interviewed me. After the interview I was hired by Mary and purchased an Avon Products start-up kit for $20.00. My first customers for Avon Products were my family, friends and messenger co-workers.

I was surprised to find that my messenger co-workers would buy Avon Products. Some of my messenger co-workers where ex-cons, tough street kids, school boys and high school athletes. It was a strange mix of youth if you asked me, but we all worked together to make sure documents were delivered on-time. I also asked the owner of Rapid Messenger Service, Peter Matthew, if I could sell Avon Products to receptionists at the companies we made deliveries to. Peter said it was ok for me to sell to receptionists, and thus I began selling a large volume of Avon Products a week.

My selling thousands of dollars of Avon Products would eventually lead to me leaving Rapid Messenger Service, but in actuality I was fired for leaving a package outside an Atlantic Record office on 6th Avenue and 51st street in Rockefeller Center. I was tired of messenger work and I didn't want to bring the package home. Peter Matthew, the owner of Rapid Messenger Service, was upset about my decision and fired me on the spot when I came in the next morning. Ed Harrington, my dispatcher, wanted Peter to let me stay, but Peter insisted I be let go; this was in 1994. By the time I got fired from Rapid Messenger Service I already had a list of offices in Manhattan that I could cold-call to sell Avon Products. With this office list I began selling Avon

Products full-time. I started grossing over $4,000 a month in sales and winning Avon Products sales awards for that effort.

The messenger business started moving further from my mind and my entrepreneur spirit really began to kick in. In the next 6 years I would be involved in a myriad of marketing projects in addition to working for Avon Products full time. I worked with many African-American related start-up enterprises and some internet based start-ups. I worked with BET Weekend Magazine, Upscale Magazine, Heritage Checks, BET Movies, Spat Films/"ILL Gotten Gains" starring Djimon Hounsou, A&B Book Distributors, Just Us Books, Cushcity. com, Confetti Entertainment Company, The Film Foundry, "Louisville" starring André Braugher, R S Entertainment now called Rocky Mountain Pictures, Inner City Entertainment, now Meridian Entertainment Group, Urban World Film Festival, Forty Acres and A Mule Filmworks, Syncopated Productions "Another Planet" a film directed by Christine Brown from Canada and Pahni Production "Tanabess" an Italian film directed by Luisa Pretolani. My start-up film releasing service called BMC Film Releasing was listed in Box Office Magazine and Hollywood Resource Directory. I look back on it as an amazing period in my life.

Around the year 2000 my Avon Products sales were declining rapidly. My telephone stopped ringing and my customers weren't ordering from Avon Products' catalogs that I brought every week to their offices. By this time I had grossed over $200,000 in Avon Products sales. Also during this 6 year period I borrowed around $20,000 to finance my many entrepreneur projects under the company name Boone Marketing Company. My Avon Products sales continue to decline just as my loans were coming due, and the Boone Marketing Company projects still weren't generating much in revenue. The most I made with Boone Marketing Company in one year was about $5,000 for distributing "ILL Gotten Gains", a million production.

In late 2000, I decided to go back to messenger work. I didn't want to give up on Boone Marketing Company becoming a successful business and being a successful entrepreneur. I knew doing messenger work would allow me the best chance to be an entrepreneur. In November of 2000 I began working for Excel Messenger Service as a part-time messenger. Around March of 2001 I began to work for Excel Messenger Service full-time, while continuing to look for solid entrepreneurial projects . . . but I wasn't finding much.

As I wrote about earlier, in the Introduction and the chapter on Excel Messenger Service, while I was doing messenger work for Excel, I started noticing a lot of people, including school children, carrying messenger bags, and I saw youth wearing a "messenger look"—a rough look that encompasses a torn or worn garment that has an authentic street feel. Along with carrying a messenger bag, I saw that it was becoming a chic fashion style for people to have nappy hair, wear worn or distressed jeans, worn or new sneakers, a worn or distressed t-shirt and really showcase the complete road warrior look of working messengers.

After denying it for a while, I finally had to admit that what I was seeing was real. On a messenger run in Queens I came across some elementary school kids going to school. I saw a school kid carrying a big messenger bag that was almost bigger than him. From that moment on, I believed that messenger styles were real. So for me as a real messenger, with a background and education in business and marketing, I sensed an opportunity to create an authentic messenger styles company. I needed an original name that would identify with real messenger culture, so I came up with the name Messenger 841. The number 841 was my messenger code at Excel Messenger Service. I talked to some of my designer friends from Avon Products, Sheila Hayes from the Gap and Linda Logan of Jones Apparel Group about my fashion idea. They thought it was a cool idea to try out. So I started working with freelance designers to help me make samples.

The first company I worked with was in New Jersey, Boneman Apparel, which made the first Messenger 841 samples including a hat and a t-shirt with "Messenger 841" written out using a transfer. In August of 2001 I attended the New York International Gift Show where I met other manufacturers. One manufacturer who was impressed with my idea was Wildwood Productions. Sharon Hendley was a vice president at Wildwood Productions who liked the messenger styles idea and was aware of this new trend in fashion.

Then—just days later—came September 11, 2001, a day that would change New York City and American history forever. I was home watching Squawk Box on CNBC-TV. When I turned to Squawk Box the first plane had already hit one of the Twin Towers. I woke my brother Freddie up and my mother up to watch what going on TV. My brother Freddie worked for PATH and I was working for Getty Images as an outside messenger. PATH and Getty Images were both located at Ground Zero. If the terrorist attacks had happened later that afternoon, my brother Freddie and I might have been directly in contact with the September 11 attack.

My cousin Anne Sealey who worked for Goldman Sachs was directly affected because she was working that morning at the New York Stock Exchange. My cousin Stephanie Wilson's husband, Robert (they live in Maryland) worked at the Pentagon, but he happened not to be at work that day. While me, my brother and mother where watching Squawk Box, we watched the second plane hit the other tower live on television. It was so surreal to all three of us. I called Excel Messenger Service about coming to work later that afternoon. Octavia, the dispatcher at Excel, said not to come into city for work.

When the attacks on September 11 at World Trade Center occurred, I was on the verge of breaking through on several of my entrepreneurial projects that would have provided enough income and profits for me to live on my earnings from Boone Marketing Company. Instead, my entrepreneurial income collapsed as well as my business loans totaling almost $20,000. I was starting to be in financial trouble, so I decided to leave Excel Messenger Service for short term assignment with Macy's Herald Square store during the Christmas Holiday Season. After the Macy's temporary job I got hired by Mitch, a manager at Kangaroo Couriers.

Kangaroo Couriers offered more commission than Excel Messenger Service, but even so, this job was paying barely enough to live on or pay down my debt. So by March of 2002 I resolved to not open any new credit accounts and work only on paying off my debt. To do this, I arranged a strict payment planned with my creditors. Some of my creditors were Beneficial, Chase Manhattan Bank, Aspire Visa, Provident Visa, AT&T Cellular, Verizon, Capital One and HSBC. In August 2002 I attended the New York International Gift Show again, this time securing deals with some of the exhibitors as a designer and sales representative. I secured manufacturing deals for my New York City tourist apparel line called Kurt Boone Authentic New York with Wildwood Productions and TYCA Corp.

I also developed a sales broker deal with Big Apple Enterprises, where I would bring in new accounts for Big Apple Enterprises to service as a manufacturer's representative. I would get override commissions from the manufacturer, based on how much Big Apple Enterprises sold. My first big broker account for Big Apple Enterprises was with C & I Collectibles, a distributor of Major League Baseball, NFL, NBA and NHL trading cards and plagues. My monthly commission from C & I Collectibles helped me pay down my debt.

I had been at Kangaroo Couriers for less than a year when I realized that messenger commissions weren't enough to pay my bills. So in early 2003 I began to look else where for higher messenger commissions while I continued to increase sales from my entrepreneur projects. Between my rent, living expenses, and paying down debt, my monthly expenses were almost $1400. Since I was barely making $300 a week at Kangaroo Couriers, and commissions from C & I Collectibles were around $200—$300 a month depending on what season of the year, I had no extra cash to save or for that matter money for health and dental insurance. The battle for me to be an entrepreneur was very hard, with creditors constantly calling me for their money. So in April of 2003 I began to work for Mobile Parcel Carriers, located in Hell's Kitchen section in Manhattan.

Mobile Parcel Carriers had a reputation in the messenger industry of being highest paying messenger commission company. It was known to pay foot messengers $300—$700 a week and bicycle messengers $400—$1000 a week. By the time I started at Mobile, messenger styles were still gaining ground in the fashion industry. There was even a book published called "Messenger Styles" that captured the trend in photographs.

I continued to have samples made for Messenger 841 Project. I signed a three-year licensing agreement with Wildwood Productions for my Zip Code T-shirt design collection and had a verbal agreement with TYCA Corp. to manufacture embossed apparel.

While working on my start-up apparel line, I was on my seventh year as a full time messenger. I had become considerably streetwise in getting around business districts of New York City, completing messenger runs very fast and efficiently. At Mobile Messenger Service, I would soon become one of their fastest foot messengers. I also started to attend the Licensing Show to try and license my Messenger 841 brand.

As soon as I entered the New York Tourist market with my apparel line, I learned that my wholesale price was too high and would limit my sales to a few stores who would sell my t-shirt designs. One of the stores who consistently sold my designs was the Phantom of Broadway stores. Phantom of Broadway stores was a Times Square-based chain of souvenir stores. One of the immediate benefits of me working for Mobile Messenger Service was being able to set my own time schedule. This allowed me to work on many projects and continue to have a steady income. By 2003, Boone Marketing Company had survived 6 years.

In 2004 I continued writing about my experiences as a messenger in the form of poetry. I introduced Sharon Hendley of Wildwood Productions to Max Rodriguez of the Harlem Book Fair, and brokered a deal for Wildwood Productions to manufacture souvenir t-shirts for the Harlem Book Fair. The Harlem Book Fair had Synthia Saint James, a famous artist, do the logo design. I was also responsible for selling t-shirts at Harlem Book Fair in addition to serving on their board of advisors as merchandise manager.

At Mobile Parcel Carriers I started meeting some of the top bicycle messengers in the city and they introduced me to New York Bicycle Messenger Association. Wil Wiechter, a co-worker at Mobile, would be my point person in helping me learn about the cycling messenger community and the Alleycat scene, where bicycle messengers race each other to see who is the fastest bicycle messenger in the city. In 2004 I also met Matthew Magnozzi of Forest Saver, who was selling messenger bags and t-shirts for the official licensed subway line by Prak Productions, owned by Lynn Lambert. Later, I would also open a sales rep account with subway line.

In 2005 I exhibited at my first trade show as an apparel designer. Matthew of Forest Saver and I split the booth fee for Surf Expo in Virginia Beach. At Surf Expo I had my samples from Wildwood Productions and TYCA Embossed, and Matthew had the Subway Line. Matthew drove his car from New York City to Virginia Beach; riding with us was Jason Felker from Canada, who came along to help Matthew and me. I had fun and learned a lot about the apparel business, but I didn't sell anything. As an entrepreneur I continued to seek new business. At the New York Gift Show in 2005 I meet Debbie Feldstein, the president of Kings International, which manufactures New York souvenirs; they also considered selling my New York designs.

I also met Mr. Kim, president of Kiat USA, a distributor and manufacturer of New York City souvenirs. Mr. Kim hired me as a marketing consultant, and also tried to sell my New York City tourist t-shirt designs. My New York City t-shirts designs weren't that bad, it was just that my wholesale prices were too high. It seems that wholesale prices for goods made in America were too high for their own New York City souvenir stores. Most New York City souvenir distributors were having their goods made overseas, so a miniature Statue of Liberty was made in China, not New York City or any other American city.

My entrepreneur spirit continued to grow, and 2006 was a busy year for me. First I signed a trade show contract for apparel with Atlanta Apparel Mart to exhibit for one year at the Alpha Show. I made three trips to Atlanta, Georgia with my Messenger 841 apparel and Kurt Boone Authentic New York samples. I mainly signed on to the trade show for exposure and not sales. I felt Messenger 841 wasn't ready for sales and demand for messenger styles was spotty at best. The Alpha Show was very strong on Hip Hop fashion and off-price urban apparel, but could do wonders to expose messenger culture to a broader audience. Messenger bag sales were fairly strong in the fashion marketplace, but the fashions of messenger culture was non-existent. It would be a great challenge to me to bring messenger fashion to market.

Even though my booth was paid for the fourth Alpha Show, I didn't attend, but I did fulfill my contract agreement. I also brokered a manufacturing deal between Vision Embroidery and Kings International. I met Vinne Luthra, the president of Vision Embroidery, on my messenger route when I passed by his shop one day on a messenger run. We discussed doing business together and I was able to broker a deal with Kings International.

By 2006 I had paid off some of my debt that I had incurred after September 11. I was still using the money I earned from Mobile Parcel Carriers to finance new projects with Boone Marketing Company. In 2007 I was about complete the foundation for building Boone Marketing Company. I had achieved success with many projects over the previous 8 years and generated sales totaling over $500,000. So instead of continuing to build experience and credibility that I had already accomplished, I decided to direct my attention to building income for me and significant profits for the company.

Then I learned there was a family farm in the family that was based in Georgia. So I contacted Ophelia Gaines, who was my cousin, at H. Kennedy Farms about my writing and marketing services. Handy Kennedy, a descendant of the founder of H. Kennedy Farms and another cousin of mine, called me and invited me down to see the farm in Cobbtown, Georgia.

At my own expense, I flew down to Atlanta over a weekend to see the farm. Cobbtown, Georgia is 3 hours drive from Atlanta and so when I arrived, Handy and his brother picked me up at the airport and drove me to the farm, and then drove me back on that Saturday. I slept over at Handy house, got up Sunday morning and went to Church in Atlanta, had lunch with cousin Frieda, and then got on a plane to go back to New York City. I was impressed with what the Kennedy Family had built. It was interesting to me that the Kennedy Family Farm had survived over 100 years and had grown to over 1000 acres.

After visiting H. Kennedy Farm and seeing what the Kennedy family was initiating with their idea of becoming a resort destination, I thought the Kennedy Farm could become a brand of authentic southern food by becoming a food packaging company. The private label food industry was growing and there was great demand for ethnic foods. The private label food business would be a perfect match for a family farm that had lasted over 100 years. So I was elated that something I had built would actually help someone in my family who needed professional marketing services.

At Mobile Parcel Carriers my commission checks were getting smaller and I started becoming afraid that if Boone Marketing Company didn't start generating more revenue I would be in trouble financially and in my marketing career. I was 47 years old with no significant assets. I had completed a large number of independent projects that looked good on my resume, but didn't generate cash flow or consistent revenue because I never had an ownership stake. After I completed each project, I would have to start all over again.

By the end of 2007 I had also become a prolific writer, having completed over 10 unpublished manuscripts. So in 2007 I worked hard to have some of these manuscripts published. Since messenger culture was popular, I started writing a lot about messenger life in poetry and essays. I partnered with Amy Bolger, Greg Ugalde and Kevin Bolger from the New York Alleycat scene and self-published a photobook called "New York Alleycats" about bike messenger racing. In addition I partnered with John Sarsgard, a photographer, on a photo essay book about Grand Central Terminal. As a messenger I always had a great love for Grand Central Terminal.

Making these photo books successful was greatly enhanced by Robert Gore Jr. of Bob Gore Productions. Robert Gore Jr. was a professional photographer and marketing consultant who supported me in all my photo-based projects. I also got a great deal of support from Fastback Creative Books who designed all my photo-based books. My writing abilities may be my blessing in disguise as I hope this will bring me residual income.

As I wrote about earlier, In the beginning of 2008 I found myself in the hospital with a blood infection. I felt sick in December 26, 2007 and was taken to emergency room on December 27 at North Shore Franklin Hospital. I was in bad shape with blood infection and case of pneumonia. I spent 29 days in the hospital and required an operation before I could start doing messenger work again. My commissions were still going down at Mobile Parcel Carriers, but my writing and marketing projects were still in place. All I needed to do was build revenue and income. I was down to two major loans of $10,000 and $5,000 being paid off entirely; all I had left to deal with was a small student loan and a small loan from Chase Manhattan Bank.

I went back to work for Mobile Parcel Carriers in February of 2008. My 2008 marketing projects include release of "On The Subway" Poetry by Kurt Boone, completing my memoir "Asphalt Warrior" and working on a book entitled "Urban Theory" by Noreen Mallory and Kurt Boone, introduction by Stephanie Wilson and Tonya Leigh, a graphic designer. I worked with the Harlem Book Fair and Author Solutions on the Wordclay book publishing platform for African-American writers. I also assisted another cousin, Lawrence Sealey, in marketing development of his uncle Herbie Nichols, a jazz pianist, who was best known for writing "Lady Sings The Blues" for Billie Holiday. I also worked on a few book projects for Robert Gore Jr. entitled "Good News From Haiti" and "Let Our Rejoicing Rise"

In 2008 I also had a few new ideas to implement in co-producing "Courier Streets", a messenger documentary film with Studio 108, and creating a signature messenger bag using my name with Seagull Bags. In addition, Ian of Chicken Switch, a boutique action sports agency, was able to secure three pairs of Converse Sneakers for me to wear from Converse Advertising. By the end of 2008 I had been a messenger full-time over 13 years. I was 48 years old and still working the city business districts as a messenger with an entrepreneur spirit.

Messenger Poet

MESSENGER POET IS A SMALL COLLECTION OF POETRY that I wrote on the subway while doing my messenger work. I have written hundreds of poems on the subway over the 12 years I have been working as a messenger.

I first started writing poetry in my senior year in high school. All throughout my childhood I had a dream of being a freelance writer. I greatly admired freelance African-American journalist and former major league baseball player, Joe Black, and every time I read one of his columns in a newspaper, I said to myself I wanted to write an opinion column when I grew up.

I found poetry to be an easy writing style to break into freelance journalism. Poetry also served as a good writing medium to described my youth, my family and my friends. My friends grew up on TV shows like "Different Strokes", "The Brady Brunch", "Green Hornet", "Fat Albert" and the "Andy Griffith Show". These TV shows where very popular that didn't involve gang life, drug dealers or black-on-black crime.

However, my urban style poetry was driven by gang life, drug dealing and black-on-black crime that was manifesting itself all around me. I set out to create a poetry style of using words to create imagery that was upfront, bold, awkward and realistic. I read Langston

Hughes, Nikki Giovanni, Maya Angelou, James Baldwin and Gwendolyn Brooks. Those African-American writers were gracious in their protest writings. They wrote about a people that were justified in having a civil rights movement. But what was happening with the youth on my block and across many other American inner cities was criminal, not legitimate protest. For me to write protest essays such as what James Baldwin could do was nearly impossible for me. Thus I decided to use poetry to express my experiences.

Fast forward from 1977 to 2002 I wrote what you would call protest poems, of which many are still unpublished. In 2001 I started to write poetry about messenger life. Writing poetry about messenger life was so incredibly fun. Writing poetry about New York City as it relates to messenger life gave me the opportunity to explore all aspects of the city, from riding the subway to walking down Park Avenue. I also continued to read other African-American poets of my generation like Rita Dove, Major Jackson, Elizabeth Alexander, Natasha Trethewey, and listen to spoken word artists including Roger Bon-Air, Reggie Gaines, Kevin Powell and Saul Williams. I even got know Bruce George, a co-creator of Def Poetry Jam.

For the last 8 years I have concentrated on writing poems about messenger life. In 2008 I published a poetry book entitle "On The Subway" with illustrations by Jeff Hill and Greg Ugalde. Then in 2010 I published the book "Messenger Poet" with illustrations by Greg Ugalde. In June 2010 I went out to San Francisco for a series of poetry readings hosted by Ink Publishing and Timbuk 2.

Using digital video I recently started producing an original web series called "The Messenger Poet Show", which simply shows me performing my poetry in various streets locations around the city, with the performance of each poem being a single segment. I also started a short-form documentary series called "Messenger Poet" describing my life as a messenger through poetry readings, city locations and interviews.

To help me in the development of these poetry video ideas, I enlisted the help of professional filmmakers. My first Messenger Poet video, entitled "Manhattan", was shot and directed by Jack Hartmann with cinematography by Graham Copeland of Studio 108 in Richmond, VA, in the summer of 2009. I started working with Alan Lebow Production, also in 2009, on the documentary series "Messenger Poet". In June of 2010 I worked on a "Messenger Poet" segment in a Sweet Corn Studio production called "Career Courier". Then in July of 2010 I worked with videographer Carl Weston on "The Messenger Poet Show", shooting 10 segments at The High Line Park in the meatpacking district of New York City. "The Messenger Poet Show" can be watched at themessengerpoet.com, themessengerpoetshow. blip.tv, filmannex.com and blip.tv.

I write my poetry on the fly as a messenger; wherever I get the inspiration to write, I will do so. I could be running into the streets on a delivery and I might stop in a safe place to write down my thoughts, or on bus rides, or best of all I write poems on my subway runs as I travel around the city on messenger jobs.

In this chapter, on one page I have my original poem, unedited in script and raw language from the notebook that I carry to track my messenger jobs, then on the facing page I have the edited and typed version of the poem. This part of my messenger life is in poetry, better known as "Messenger Poet".

Alvin Ailey Dancer
by Kurt Byrne

Keeping the urban
Aesthetic Fire burning
There so meaning
in Dance

Dancing to
Drum Beats
In Cities of
Concrete, Cars,
airplanes and
people congestion

Alvin Ailey 2023
is so remix

ALVIN AILEY

Keeping the urban dance
movement going. There is
so much meaning in dance.
Dancing to drum beats
in a city of concrete
sidewalks, skyscrapers, cars,
airplanes, subway cars
and people congestion.
Alvin Ailey 2003 is in the mix.

KOBE   7-10-03
by Kurt Boone

My newspaper read
sexual assault
in Colorado

Daily News, New
York City
Front page

I don't believe it
As to victim my
respect and love
is paramount

KOBE

My newspaper I am reading said

Kobe Bryant committed a sexual

assault in Colorado. It was on front page of

Daily News in New York City. I don't believe it. As to victim

my respect

and love goes out to you. But for you Kobe

I hope it is a

misunderstanding and

that the charges against

you are not true. Walked by NBA Headquarters

today as messenger number: 300 Book

of Mobile Parcel Carriers. My love for game of basketball

is unquestion. I hope the charges

against you isn't true, Kobe

RAO's
by Kurt Borne

Murder at RAO's
Wented in Harlem
yesterday, Monday
December 22.

At Cosmetypo's
Secret RAO
carry an exclusive
guest list

A normance average person,
couldn't get a seat
at the upscale

RAO'S

Murder at Rao's located in

Harlem New York yesterday,

Monday December 22. Al Capone types eat at

Rao's. Rao's has an exclusive

guest list. A normal person wouldn't

be able to get a seat at Rao's,

a upscale restaurant. America the beautiful

America the ugly

my food is chised

Rap Wars
by Kurt Borne

Nas vs Jay Z
Tupac vs Notorious BIG
Little Kim vs Foxy Brown

So So Def
Bow Wow
It's Like Mike

murder inc records
Rockefella records
Def Jam Records
Death Row Records
Jive Records

RAP WARS

Nas vs. Jay Z

Tupac vs Notorious BIG

Little Kim vs Foxy Brown So So Def

Bow Wow is like Mike Murder Inc Records

Rockefella Records

Def Jam Records

Death Row Records

Jive Records Hot 97 on your radio

Power 105 FM on your radio

RAP WARS

As messenger 300 Book for Mobile Parcel Carriers

On the streets of midtown Manhattan.

Not on a power lunch but hustling.

RAP WARS

⑥ Curious for life
        by Kent Bare

Though the electrified
airless tunnel; And by
big business lives me
If I am to being a messenger
slicing through city traffic
at blinding speed on my
bicycle, is the sweetest
        thing.
Though the money at night
I am a curious for life,

COURIER FOR LIFE

Though the dispatcher
ain't my friend. And
big business loves me.

It's fun being a messenger
slicing through city traffic
at blinding speed on my
bicycle.

It is the sweetest thing.

Though the money ain't right
I am a courier for life.

People
by Kurt Boone

F Train
4-14-06
7:24pm

Riding F Train to
go home I see
People

A father
A son
A daughter
A sister
A uncle
A Neice
A Nephew
A Grandfather
A Husband

PEOPLE

Riding F train to go home

I see people A father

A son

A daughter

A sister

A uncle

A niece

A nephew

A grandmother

A husband

A wife

A brother

A grandfather

A mother

A cousin New York City my hometown

Missery on Aesthetics
By Kurt Bane

Union Chorus
As I see what I do
everyday, this is what it is
Down Wall Street
on Fifth Avenue
and Sixth Avenue
and the Eastside
and the Westside
Pushing Packages
down City Streets
Union Chorus
messege As it is

8:30 am
5:18 09
083 parcents
210 that

KB

MESSENGER AESTHETICS

Urban Chaos

As I see what I do everyday.
This is what it is.

Down on Wall Street
and on Fifth Avenue
and on Sixth Avenue

On the eastside
and on the westside

Pushing packages
down city streets.

Urban Chaos

Messenger aesthetics

Going Downtown
By Lento Bone

Getting there messages
Work Going downtown, it's
bad. Not because of September
11 but there no work going
uptown, and when there is.
no work, you don't get paid
Nevertheless.
I Remember
Wounded Knee
Hiroshime Hiroshima
nagasaki Nagasaki
and now
September 11

GOING DOWNTOWN

Getting messenger worked
going downtown is sometimes
a bad job.

Not because of
September 11,
but because there is
no worked going uptown.

And when there is no worked,
you don't get paid.

Nevertheless
I remember

Wounded Knee
Hiroshima

Nagasaki

and now September 11.

My American Dream or

is it Friday the 13th ?

THE GOLDEN BIKE

Cycling is golden
As I love to ride
It's about time you recognize.

Cruisers
Fixies
Roadies
Mountain biking and
bicycle motor cross.

You know the scene
Critical Mass
Alleycats
Velodrome Racing
and the Peel Sessions.

Bike lanes all around the world.

Cycling is golden

As I love to ride

It's about time you recognize.

The Golden Bike
By Kurt Barno

cycling is golden
I love to ride
It's about time you realize

cruisers
fixie
recliner
mountain bikes
and the bmx bicycle
and cross

you know the scene
crucial mass
alleycats
velodrome
and track sessions
The Golden Bike

About the author

KURT BOONE IS A NATIVE NEW YORKER. HE IS THE author of seven books, most notably co-author of *New York Alleycats* with photography by Amy Bolger, and *Messenger Poet* with illustrations by Greg Ugalde. Kurt has been profiled in *The New York Times*, *New York Daily News* and *Courier Magazine*. In his fifteen years as a courier, Kurt has made important deliveries for former President of the United States Bill Clinton, New York City Police Commissioner Raymond Kelly, HBO Sopranos Production, designer Ralph Lauren, Jazz at Lincoln Center, Alvin Ailey American Dance Theater, comedian Bill Cosby and legendary newsman Walter Cronkite. Kurt is the founder of two small businesses, Boone Marketing Company and the Messenger 841 Project. He has also collaborated in designing a professional messenger bag with Seagull Bags. He recently produced the original web series "The Messenger Poet Show" and is also an avid supporter of urban cycling.

Acknowledgments

THIS BOOK COULD NOT HAVE BEEN COMPLETED WITH-out the support of many individuals; I am greatly appreciative of their support. The entire Boone Family for their total support of my writing projects. In addition I would like to thank a few by name: Stephanie Wilson, PhD; my editor Denise Hidalgo; my book designer Mark Melnick; Amy Bolger; John Sarsgard; Bob Gore; Mobile Parcel Carriers; Book Mobile; Chicken Switch; Oliver Werner; Sarah Meskin; New York Bicycle Messenger Foundation; and my product sponsors Wildwood Productions; TYCA Corp; Vision Embroidery; Kiat USA; Timbuk 2; Converse Sneakers; Manhattan Portage; Seagull Bags; Function Drinks; Chrome Bags and Blaq Design.